# WISDOM WHISPERER

## An Insider's Secrets from her 20s, 30s, and 40s for Success as a Business Executive

by Kathleen E.R. Murphy

# WISDOM WHISPERER

Wordsmith: Kathleen Veth

Design and Composition: Cheryl L. Cromer
Square Moon Publishing Solutions LLC
Square-Moon.com

## | Acknowledgements |

Carol Agranat, Brian Babineau, Robert Thieron Badger, Peter Baldwin,
Lauren Balliveau, Babson College, Beyoncé, Big Brothers Big Sisters of America,
The Boys & Girls Clubs, David Bowie, Richard Branson, Andrew Brearton,
Monique Tremblay Burke, Captain Dan and the Crew of of Falla (FallaReefTrips.au),
Dr. Pauline R. Clance, Dr. Donald Clifton, Marlene Gasdia-Cochrane, Cheryl Cromer,
Dalai Lama, Greg DeGuglielmo, Richard Delahaye, Epictetus, Michele Equale,
Malcolm Forbes, FindAMentor.com, First Landing Resort, Lautoka, Fiji,
Mahatma Gandhi, Gail Goodman, Misty Grennell, Habitat for Humanity,
Michael Hanifan, Mike Howell, Gary Huffnagle, Dr. Suzanne A. Imes,
Mick Jagger, Stephanie Jimenez, Dwayne "The Rock" Johnson, Bill Keane,
Doug Kennedy, Tim Kenny, Blair LaCorte, Holden Laquerre, Torin Michael Lekan,
"Lie to Me"/Netflix, Matt McCarthy, Thomas Merton, Maureen Electa Monte,
Daniel I. Murphy, Emily R. Murphy, Thomas Nelders, Nike, Kathy Leslie Peluso,
Zak Pines, Quantas Airlines - Elfie, Tom Rath, Anthony Santiago,
Jill Schmidt, Bronwyn Shinnick, Cole Shinnick, Maxwell Shinnick, Stephen Shinnick,
Lou Shipley, Simon Sinek, Patrick Sweeney, Tina Turner, University of Maine (Orono),
Kathleen Veth, Matthew Whitlock, Oscar Wilde, Serena Williams, Oprah Winfrey,
Kate Winslet, Sean Wright, and Women Unlimited

## | About the Author |

Market Me Too Founder and CEO/CMO, Kathleen E.R. Murphy is known for radiating enthusiasm and positive energy. Her marketing career has spanned more than 20 years, and has been focused on technology and start-up companies in a variety of industries.

Kathleen, a Certified Gallup Strengths Coach, is well-regarded for her global marketing leadership and partnership marketing acumen, and has been sought after for her innovative, collaborative, and strategic thinking style by companies such as Barracuda Networks, Constant Contact, Dell/EMC, Hitachi, and Staples. She is an inspirational public speaker who is often tapped to share her motivational wisdom about life as a female executive in the high-tech business workplace.

Kathleen's highly creative problem solving and entrepreneurial approach to growing companies has served her well in dynamic, fast-paced environments. She has mastered the art of building "best-in-class" marketing teams, and credits her family lineage as inventors and entrepreneurs for shaping her career path.

Kathleen lives in Chelmsford, Massachusetts, with her husband and three children. To learn more about Market Me Too and how Kathleen can help your company, email her at KathyMurphy@me.com or visit MarketMeToo.net

# WISDOM WHISPERER
## Insider Secrets for Business Success

### | Table of Contents |

## Chapter 3 | Life

## Chapter 4 | Tips & Resources

# | Introduction |

*My "Why," or how I overcame Imposter Syndrome and leveraged my positivity strength to become an entrepreneur.*

Why did I write this book? The simple answer? I have wanted to write a book for many years. I feel I have something to offer and am eager to whisper my wisdom to anyone who wants to listen.

The more complicated reason is that I've been holding myself back. Why? Because I was afraid. After years of soul searching and talking to women around the globe, I believe my fear is due to a phenomenon with which many females struggle — the Imposter Syndrome.

The Imposter Syndrome was coined in 1978 by clinical psychologists Pauline R. Clance and Suzanne A. Imes. It describes high-achieving individuals marked by an inability to internalize their accomplishments and a persistent fear of being exposed as a fraud.

This is why it has taken me over 30 years to put pen to paper — or fingers to keyboard.

What had I been thinking about all these years as a woman, wife, mother of three, high-tech executive, mentor, coach, and now entrepreneur? And what did I need to share?

About a year ago, I set out to re-tool or reinvent myself professionally. I was not feeling authentic. I knew I wanted — needed — to leverage my instinctual abilities.

According to Tom Rath's *Strengths Finder 2.0*, it turns out my greatest strength is being positive. Unfortunately, the majority of my professional career has not allowed me to fully engage this strength until recently, when an opportunity presented itself at an unlikely place — a male-dominated software company in the Northeast.

The challenge was to turn around a sales team that had not met its goal in 11 months. The secondary challenge was to act as a bridge between this team and the marketing department.

Fast forward six weeks: The sales team exceeded its projections for the first time all year.

How did this happen? Was it a miracle, or a repeatable model? The answer is multi-dimensional, but boils down to this: I kept the complete focus on my greatest strength — positivity. My positive attitude encouraged a team of a dozen employees to believe they could achieve what had been an elusive goal.

This achievement inspired me to want to do this for other teams and individuals. More importantly, it provided me with the direction for which I was soul searching.

I no longer felt like a fraud or imposter.

I am now eager to harness my positivity to help others define and reach their goals.

Better yet, I am able to enjoy my life every day while earning a living helping and encouraging others to believe in themeselves — which does not seem like work to me (which is the best part)!

I am the Wisdom Whisperer. I hope you enjoy my book!

# Chapter 1 | Work

## Articulating Your Value Proposition

*Everyone has a personal Value Proposition — that innovation, service, or feature intended to make a company or product attractive to customers. Have you written yours yet? If not, here's why you need to do so, and how to write it.*

No matter who you are, what industry you work in, if you are just starting out in your career, or have worked for more than 20 years, you should be able to articulate your Value Proposition. Another common term associated with this is called an "Elevator Pitch." Both can be utilized personally or professionally. Let's focus on the development of your personal Value Proposition, and why you should create one.

The first reason is to be able to verbally showcase your talents when anyone asks, "What do you do?" Even if they are not entirely interested in hearing what you have to say, or are simply asking to be polite, you never know if what you are conveying to the person you are speaking with might be giving you an opportunity to make an impact, either personally or professionally.

For example, let's say you are at your friend's graduation party and are speaking with another guest. The two of you have at least one person in common — the graduate, and the person you are speaking with happens to be at a "hot" start-up that is hiring 100 people this year. After hearing your Value Proposition, the other guest asks if you are interested in learning more about their company as your background sounded perfectly aligned to several of the open positions. This type of interaction happens frequently; but too often, people are not prepared to take advantage of the opportunity because they have not created their Value Proposition to share with others.

Another reason to create your personal Value Proposition is to be able to readily converse with others on a general topic relating to how you spend your time and energy. Granted, you might not be working at your dream job right now, but perhaps you are working towards developing the skills to go after your ideal career role.

Your personal Value Proposition describes your ultimate goals. The people you meet might be able to help you get one step closer to your ideal dream job or company. People like to help other people, especially when they present themselves open to assistance and a desire to network with others who can potentially help them pursue the new direction they are working towards.

The final reason to craft your personal Value Proposition is to share with others your own story and journey related to where you are personally or professionally.

By nature, most people are curious — some more than others. Even if the person you are speaking with is only mildly curious, they will still be interested in hearing your Value Proposition. Think of your Value Proposition as a way to establish a personal connection with the person you are talking with, and by all means, make sure you ask them to tell you about their personal Value Proposition. Simply ask them how they spend their time and energy, or what keeps their interest and attention during the day. You might be pleasantly surprised by what they tell you.

Since you now know why you should have your own Value Proposition, let's get started! There are tons of Web sites that can provide you with the structure needed to begin developing and crafting your Value Proposition.

If you already have a personal Value Proposition, congratulations! Perhaps you'll be inspired to tweak it after reading this article.

After you have crafted or updated your Value Proposition, I would love to read it, so please share it with me at kathymurphy@me.com. I'll be happy to reciprocate.

## Got Culture?  (Company culture, that is.)

*Creating your company culture and making it a strong and desirable one should be a top business priority, regardless of your business size, or the industry you are in.  So why do so many companies under invest or not make it a priority to do so?*

Corporate culture refers to the beliefs and behaviors that determine how a company's employees and management interact and handle outside business transactions.  Often, corporate culture is implied, not expressly defined, and develops organically over time from the cumulative traits of the people the company hires.

I have had the good fortune of working at two of the best companies in the United States when it comes to outstanding company culture.  I credit Lou Shipley, CEO at Black Duck, and Gail Goodman, former CEO of Constant Contact, for encouraging their company cultures to be genuine, rather than contrived or mandated.  This is not easy to accomplish, and it's not by chance their corporate cultures are impressive, as they, with the help of many others, routinely work on culture development.

At Black Duck, Tim Kenny, vice president of culture, embodies how to practice and create a company culture that would make even Apple jealous.  To get a sense of Black Duck's culture, check out the YouTube videos of Tim's famous office antics.

Are technology companies the only ones that understand and embrace the importance of having an amazing corporate culture?  I hope not, but there are also industries who are well known for their lack of a healthy philosophy.  Is this a badge of honor?

The benefits of having a strong, positive corporate culture cannot be underrated.  Sure, there is a cost to creating, developing, and maintaining a healthy corporate culture, but there is more evidence to support why you should invest in upgrading your corporate culture, than not.

There are varying degrees of what effort is required to create a positive company atmosphere.  Think of creating a positive company culture as you would visiting the gym regularly as a way to remain fit and you're on the right track (pun intended). First, start slowly. Engage a select group of people in the company who are genuinely interested in making it a better and more fun place to work. This group can then meet monthly to brainstorm ideas to help develop their corporate culture.

For example, Black Duck employees make waffles every Wednesday, and call the event "Waffle Wednesday." The company invested in commercial-grade waffle irons, then assigned staff to procure the ingredients, cook, and clean up. It is a fun team-building activity, as most of the employees participate at some point during the year.

Another idea is to invite some food trucks to your parking lot, especially if you are in a large building complex. Plan brainstorming sessions around fun holidays, such as Cinco de Mayo; schedule regular sports-themed or tailgating days, where staff wear their favorite team's shirts or hats to work. Or, schedule a monthly themed activities to rally employees, such as Pizza Fridays or potluck lunches.

The bottom line is that corporate culture does not have to cost tens of thousands of dollars to support, and can make a significant contribution to helping your company retain employees because they are happy working there.

Reach out to me if you would like more low-cost, high-value ideas about boosting and building corporate culture ideas — or share your ideas. It delights me to see other companies working on improving their company culture, knowing how much fun it can be to work in an organization with an amazing corporate culture. Don't delay: Start today on making your company the one that everyone wants to work at.

*This shared wisdom is dedicated to Tim Kenny, whom I admire for his amazing creativity and talent in creating a corporate culture that would impress both Disney and Google.*

## Dress For Success (Not the "Club")

*There's a risk to dressing too casually, even when the company handbook outlines its office attire policy. Since there are potentially numerous interpretations of "business casual" attire, let's go one step further to help you not make the mistake of misinterpretation.*

*Dress for Success* — the modern equivalent of "Clothes maketh the man." These phrases articulate the belief that what you wear really does matter. "Impression management" has become part of mainstream popular psychology and business studies, with dress for success a central plank of both. It may be a cliché that you should dress for success, or "dress for the job you want, not the one you have," but every day I notice that some people clearly never received this memo. Instead, I see many who show up at work looking like they are heading immediately to either the gym, back to bed, or a night club. (I'm almost positive they are not.)

With companies adopting a more relaxed dress code, often people have taken it upon themselves to go beyond the line of what is actually an acceptable style of clothes to wear to work. Don't get me wrong — I'm all for being comfortable, but I also do not ever want to feel uncomfortable because my work attire is potentially too casual.

So, if your company has a written work attire policy, consider taking it up a notch. Why? Because it is far better than not to be perceived as being overdressed and as someone who knows how to present themselves at a level above their current role.

Most people are visually oriented. When they see someone who is dressed casually, they assume the person might not have the credibility they deserve. This is a presumptive interpretation, of course, but I have witnessed over and over again how people are treated based on the way they dress in the office. Choosing appropriate professional attire applies to both sexes, as well as to those who do not identify with one sex or the other.

Here's an illustration of how a misperception can be based on your clothing. My company was exhibiting at an industry trade show; multiple employees of all ages and genders were stationed in our booth. Everyone but me wore a company shirt and jeans.  Since I was also meeting with the press and knew I would be interacting with other exhibitors, I chose more business-oriented clothing.  While visiting our booth, attendees automatically assumed I was the CEO of the company.  I was not; but the perception people had, based on my outfit, was that I was in charge.

Now, you don't need to dress like a CEO, but here are some quick tips to avoid making the mistake of dressing too casually at work.

1. If you would wear the clothes to bed, don't wear them into the office.

2. If you would wear the clothes to the gym, save them for your workouts.

3. There may, in fact, be clothes that can nicely transition from office to night club, but if you have even the slightest hesitation about whether to wear the clothes you have selected, then don't.

4. If you have a great sense of humor, or collect T-shirts that are representative of your political, cultural, or religious views, wear these on the weekend — not to the office.

5. You may love form-fitting clothing, but if some of it rides the line of making others uncomfortable, don't wear them to the office.  This applies to both men and women.  And ladies, leave the showy cleavage tops at home — they make both men and women uncomfortable when you expose too much skin, especially in a professional setting.

If you have not been graced with good style, or are still perplexed by your company's dress code, ask one of your friends for advice, someone whom you perceive to dress well.  They will be flattered you asked, and you will increase your chances of having others in the company view you in a more positive professional manner.

The definition of dressing for success can certainly be subjective, but doing so is worth the effort.  You will be pleasantly surprised with the positive comments you receive.

And who doesn't like compliments?

# Who's Your Mentor?

*Having a business coach or mentor can make a fundamental difference in your business life. In honor of Mother's Day, I chose to write about a person many of us consider our first coach — their mom, or someone who played this role in their life.*

Everyone needs a coach, and most of us started out with one — usually a mother, father, or grandparent — someone who played an instrumental role in our formative years. Whoever your first coach or mentor was, remember to thank them for what they did for you as you were developing as a person.

The ironic thing about having a coach or mentor is we typically don't continue to have a person in our lives who plays this role as we grow into adulthood. Why not? Or are you one of the fortunate people who does?

I always wanted to have an "official" business coach or mentor. Instead, I took it upon myself to become one, first by acting as a mentor to others, then more formally by joining various organizations where I could hone my coaching skills. (A shout out to the Babson College MBA program for allowing me to mentor three of their women MBA candidates, as well as to the Women Unlimited program where, with other members, I mentor executive business women.) These and similar programs support the values associated with business coaching and mentorship.

But the concepts of coaching and mentoring can also be applied outside of the business world. Having mentored well over 100 people — many of whom still consider themselves to be a mentee 20 years later — I am a staunch supporter of the benefits associated with having a coach. I have seen how mentoring has directly and positively impacted both business as well as personal lives. Coaches challenge you; they listen well; they help guide you to meeting your goals; possess the experience required to offer emotional support when required; provide constructive feedback; and make themselves available to you when you need them the most.

Recently, I attended a Gallup seminar that shared a report that documents what millennials want in the workplace. The number one thing it cited was that millennial employees expect or desire a mentor. Since in just a few short years millennials will out number other generations in the workforce, this generation's desire for coaching intrigues me. The report also noted that presently organizations will not employ enough people who are either trained as, or want to be, a coach. How will the shortage of coach/mentors be addressed?

To surmount this challenge, millennials initially should seek outside resources to support the need for business mentoring and coaching. Start with colleges, religious associations, community groups, and professional associations.

My recent research uncovered a free association online, FindAMentor.com, that offers coaching as well as encourages new members to become mentors themselves. The organization's concept is based on paying it forward. Groups like these are excellent starting points in building your network or reaching out to mentor others.

Thank you to all the mothers, fathers, grannies, grandpas, and co-workers, and to those others who have moved on to play the instrumental role of being a coach or mentor. Continue doing what you do, as you are all making a tremendous difference.

*This story is dedicated to two amazing mothers — Terry Kuprevich, mother of Misty Grennell, and Emily R. Murphy, my mother. Thank you for being my first mentor and coach. You are still an amazing one to this day!*

## Cultivating a Social Network

*Meeting a colleague for lunch or coffee is more important than you think. Getting out of the office and onto neutral territory helps build professional relationships. Everyone eats and drinks! Capitalizing on this should not be underestimated. Get to know someone better and build a relationship one sandwich or coffee at a time.*

It might seem obvious as a relationship-building tool, but have you taken full advantage of getting to know one of your colleagues, or perhaps your boss or team, by sharing a cup of Joe or bowl of soup?

When I ask people how often they make plans to go out to lunch or coffee with co-workers, I am always surprised by how few people are. I have seen incredible transformations in a relationship following many of my social interactions.

For example, once I asked a colleague out to lunch simply to see why she was acting so negatively towards me. Some of my colleagues thought I was crazy for investing any time or energy in the relationship. Just one lunch with my coworker transformed her from being a nightmare to work with, to being one of my biggest supporters. In fact, we worked collaboratively from that point on.

What made the difference? It was actually pretty simple. She did not fully understand the work I was asking her to do, and thought it was a waste of time. What she did not realize was that it was enormously helpful to me. When she realized her work was perceived as being a valuable contribution to the business, the passive/aggressive behavior evaporated. We continued to have lunch, and actually have kept in touch since we stopped working together.

This example has not been an anomaly; I have been able to repeat similar results with almost all of the people with whom I have spent time. This simple exercise is absolutely applicable to any person in an organization. All you have to do is ask them out for coffee or lunch.

If you're the one asking, you're the one picking up the tab. If the person you've invited is your superior and wants to pay, offer to split the tab.

To get you started, here are some questions you can use to have similar results.

- Do you like to travel?  If they have not done much traveling, ask them about what three places in the world they would like to visit.

- Do you have any pets?

- Do you do any volunteer work?

- How did you choose this career?

- Would you recommend this career to others?

- Do you have a super power?

- With what character on television do you identify?

- Do you enjoy learning about topics unrelated to your profession?

- Who inspires you?

Basically, get them talking about themselves — a subject most everyone loves.  Don't be shocked by the fact they might not reciprocate.

If the conversation goes the way I predict it will — and I have years of experience with coffee and lunch outings — by the end of your meal, you will have planted the seeds to develop an entirely different relationship.

The next step in this process is to make a list of the people with whom you need to start queuing up for coffee and lunch experiences.  You can either invite them informally by talking to them and agreeing upon a date and time to get together, or you can send them an email invitation asking them when (not if) you can treat them to coffee or lunch.

The more experiences you have with socializing with the people on your list, the more opportunities you will have to expand your network, be considered an influencer, and, in general, take your career in a direction I promise it would not be headed otherwise.  What are you waiting for?  Start making a list today and sending out invitations tomorrow.  Doing so will open a whole new world of opportunities for you on your professional journey.

## Embrace Your Wierdness!

*People always tell you to be yourself, but can you really be yourself in a professional environment? Do you really know what qualities make you who you are and how to truly embrace your uniqueness? Wouldn't it be much less exhausting to have the freedom to be genuinely you? Here's how.*

Why do so many people want to emulate others or be like someone they are not? Maybe because it is more difficult or uncomfortable to simply be themselves. Maybe it looks like it's easier to imitate what someone else is doing. Lots of people do this, but they are not being true to themselves or allowing their actual talents and personality to be fully actualized.

Part of the reason people act like others is because they think they need to fit in to be accepted, or because they do not want to call too much attention to who they really are. Why wouldn't you want to fully embrace your unique self, or what I playfully call your "weirdness?"

I recently saw a Broadway show called *Dear Evan Hansen*. The story was about a teenager desperate to have others acknowledge him. He did not know how to go about this, however, and indirectly, through an action he took, got more attention and was definitely noticed, but not in the way he had anticipated. This presented a challenge he was unprepared to handle, but he managed the situation as best he could, which was via a series of lies that spiraled out of control.

Ultimately, Evan was able to get the situation back under control; but it wasn't until he realized he needed to embrace who he was as a person first. Sound familiar to an experience you may have had as a teenager?

Now fast forward to your 20s and 30s or beyond. You may still be trying to figure out how to express your true personality while simultaneously being accepted for who you really are. Allowing your true personality to shine in a professional environment is not easy, but it is possible to achieve. The trick is to be honest with yourself about who you really are.

Are you someone who is empathetic to co-workers and truly interested in collaborating with them? Or are you highly competitive and interested in getting ahead, no matter who you upset? Do you enjoy making others laugh and bring a light-hearted air to your working environment? Or, perhaps you are the creative or analytical type who wants to share these skills with your colleagues.

If you had to describe yourself in two or three words, would you be able to do so easily? Would others have an easy time describing you, or would your colleagues describe the employee you are portraying, rather than the person you really are?

So, who are the people who embrace their weirdness? In my experience, they are people who are the happiest and most successful in terms of having found what they want to be doing professionally. As Oprah might say, they are their authentic selves.

They do not look at their job as work, but rather as something they enjoy spending time doing and for which they happen to get paid. When I ask them about how they figured out how to match their interests or passions with the profession they have chosen, they often tell me the work they are doing best suits their personality. It's what makes them happy and allows them to be true to who they are.

Since most people know what type of character and temperament they have, using positive traits as a foundation to help choose your career will provide solid guidelines to allow you to truly express your personality in a professional environment. If you are currently working where you do not feel like you can be yourself, have you stopped to consider why? Are you in the right profession, or are you trying to conform to be accepted? If so, perhaps it is time to stop and reconsider.

Think about what you can do to be true to your one-of-a-kind personality and what makes you unique. When you allow yourself to be who you really are and accept and embrace your weirdness, everyone benefits.

Playwright Oscar Wilde (or perhaps influential spiritual thinker and mystic Thomas Merton — experts disagree on who) once said, "Be yourself; everyone else is already taken."

No matter the author, embrace this statement, and start seeing how much happier you can and will be, both at work and in life.

## Does Presence Matter?

*Presence. Do you have it? Do you know how to have it? Do you want it? Ultimately does it matter if you have it or not? You be the judge.*

Some people have presence — that poise and self-assurance that allows one to project a sense of ease — because they speak loudly, or because they are trying to project confidence. This is what I would refer to as having a false sense of self-assurance. Conversely, the quiet person may have the greatest presence because they have gained tenure and the trust of others based on their life experiences.

Presence can be perceived from both a physical, versus a philosophical point of view, as renowned entrepreneur and *Forbes Magazine* publisher Malcom Forbes once said, "Presence is more than just being there."

So, is it possible not to have presence? This sounds fairly philosophical, but in reality, everyone has presence. Boiling this down to the simplest concept, the difference between people is how much presence they have, and whether having presence is situational, or sustained. Another way of looking at the concept of presence is whether it differs based on gender, age, or geographic location. Taking this concept one step further, does it matter how much presence you have?

Thinking of presence as a physical concept, it may be easier to determine whether someone does or does not command a large sense of presence, or whether they simply are present. Does having presence or a greater amount of it gain you anything? I think it does.

Actual or perceived leaders, or people who are regularly around others, draw others in, simply by being themselves. They are able to influence others positively or negatively. This is likely because they possess a sense of natural charisma, or command of others' attention. People who have a sense of presence typically draw others to them; others seek them out. Either party may or may not be aware of this happening; however, the people who are drawn to the individual with presence would describe the experience as a sense of magnetic pull.

Not being a scientist, but rather a curious human being, I wonder why some people have more presence than others, and whether there are differences in the types of presence one can have.

If presence is a physical attribute, perhaps it can be gained or lost over time? If the concept of presence is also more philosophical or situationally based, are the people with presence who are not defined as leaders, leaders in the making?

In business, most leaders have a sense of presence, but there are clearly people who are not technically leaders who have a tremendous sense of presence among their peers. Or, are these non-leader individuals at a juncture of becoming leaders given the right situation, timing, and place?

If we agree everyone has presence, and it is a matter of how much on a measurement scale each person has, would you want to have an ability to gain more presence, or are you satisfied with the presence level you currently have?

To have presence, you must be fully present.

Have you given thought about whether you command a sense of presence when you are with others, or been told you have a strong sense of presence? I would enjoy hearing your thoughts about this topic, so drop me a note to let me know what you think.

## Curing the Monday Morning Blues

*Need a cure for the Monday morning blues? Who doesn't!? Learn how to make Monday a day you will actually look forward to.*

I am certain we'd all agree that there are many days you think work is a hassle and that you would not consider it a privilege to have a job, or a career. But if you do have either of these, you are lucky.

Keep this in mind on Sunday night, Monday morning, or any other day of the week you are dreading going to, or being at work. Chances are you landed your job due to the privilege of higher education, supportive parents, a roof over your head, and food on the table each day — circumstances with which not everyone in the U.S. has been blessed.

I recently spoke with an incredible woman whom I admire who works in the life insurance industry. She reminded me about how privileged we are. One of the reasons, she said, is that both of us have a college education. As we discussed the concept of privilege, she asked me if I had seen the YouTube video *Life of Privilege Explained in a $100 Race*. In the video, a coach has a diverse group of students each take a step forward for every bit of assistance they've received. Eventually, only students of color are left behind.

It was absolutely eye-opening to be reminded how something as basic as not having to worry about where I will sleep tonight, or where my next meal is coming from, can often be taken for granted. A number of the high schoolers in the video had these actual concerns.

If you fall into the privilege category, you have not likely had to give any thought to these challenges on a regular basis. Or ever. This does not mean we shouldn't, it just indicates that we probably do not understand or appreciate the struggles others have to go through simply to survive. And yes, we're talking about people in America.

How does this topic relate to your job? There is something each of us can do to help others who may not have had the same privileges we take for granted — especially those who are preparing to enter into the workforce in five or ten years.

One way to support the next generation is to set aside a few hours a week to volunteer. There are a number of organizations eager for help: The Boys & Girls Clubs, Habitat for Humanity, Big Brothers Big Sisters of America, your local middle and high schools, foster care or transitional home programs, and youth sports leagues. Choose a program whose emphasis is on youngsters between ages 12-18 — our future leaders who need all the support they can get. Providing them with guidance, knowledge, and support just may mean they will have the confidence and strength to move to the head of the dozens of lines we all face in both life and in business.

Many company executives I talk to are looking for ways to further engage their employees either during the work day, or prior to or after work. Some even allow employees to have volunteer hours count as on-the-clock time, even if they are salaried. By allowing staff to volunteer their time during work hours, everyone benefits. This may seem elementary as a concept, but it's not. And it is but one small way to help offset the privilege gap.

So, the next time you catch yourself complaining about your life, your job, or how hard everything is, think back to the YouTube video and how privilege is something more people can have if we all do our part in first recognizing the issue, and then taking action.

Everyone deserves a chance at a better life, and those who have had the fortune of privilege can make a difference in the lives of those who do not. Think about this the next time you are looking for a cure for your Monday morning blues.

## Are You "That" Person in the Office?

*Let's face it, no one is perfect; but there are varying degrees of who is easy to work with, and who is, well, not. When you are hiring people, or considering a job change, how do you tell which side of the coin a person or a company is on? There's a 50/50 chance you will end up with one or the other. The real test is learning how to discern how far they gravitate to the extreme on either end.*

Regardless of how many years you have been working, undoubtedly you have encountered both ends of the co-worker spectrum — people you enjoy working with, and those who make you want to hit the eject button if there were one. Fortunately, most people fall into the mid-range of being good to work with.

Most people do their best to keep drama out of the workplace, but some either do not realize they are doing this, or simply can't help themselves. Sometimes it might be a phase the person is going through, which makes it seem like every day is filled with their unnecessary drama.

But what if you are one of the complicated/messy people everyone dreads working with, or if you are managing someone like that? Chances are you want to figure out how to deal with someone who is complicated to help make your working experience as gratifying as possible. The best approach is to ask them a few questions. Here is what I recommend:

- How would you rate your daily interaction satisfaction rate with your colleagues on a scale of one to five, with five being the highest?
- What is the best part of your day, excluding coffee breaks, lunch, and leaving the office. (P.S. If those are the highlights, that's a big red flag.)
- If money did not matter, what would be your ideal job?
- Who do you admire professionally, and why?

The answers will allow you to have an open dialogue. If they are clearly not happy, encouraging them to think about what they need to do to make interacting with the people more enjoyable is a good place to start.

If you do not manage the person you are having the conversation with, ask the questions — being empathetic to their situation could be the catalyst to turn their attitude around.

If you are a hiring manager building your dream team, here are some questions you can ask to ensure you find people you will not regret hiring:

- How important are celebrating your colleagues birthdays to you on a scale of one to five, with five being the highest rating?

- Tell me about your most recent social service experience; what was the best part?

- What kinds of teams were you on growing up? This can include being in a band, on the debate team, in a choir or the drama club, and not just sports teams. (Never being on a team might indicate they have limited experience with collaborative experiences.)

- What is an example of an accomplishment you are most proud of?

- Tell me about things that motivate you to be kind to others.

- Have you ever had a service job (bartending, waiting tables, candy striper, camp counselor)? (I have generally only hired people who say *yes* to this question, as it demonstrates they know how to serve the needs of others first, and interact well with people.)

- What is one or more things about which you are passionate? (They do not have to be work related.)

- On a scale of one to five, with five being the highest rating, how important is it for people to get along?

- When you walk into a room, how would others know you have arrived?

Since most people will be working for a large majority of their lives, it is imperative to have strategies in place to find the right people and companies to work with and for. Life is too short to work with "that" person.

## The Super Power of Persistence

*Persistence is a Super Power. You may or may not have it now, but you can get it if you try!*

A quality I have often admired in others is their persistence, and their ability to apply their perseverance and focus both on the job, and outside of work. People who are persistent seemingly have a plan, and they typically execute it and get results. Do you know someone like this? Is this one of your super power traits, or do you wish you were more persistent?

Is being persistent an innate quality, or is it one that can be developed? Is it also possible to be more persistent in some situations versus others, as you could be more motivated to persist towards a particular goal — for example, getting in shape for the summer, going after a promotion at work, organizing and cleaning your home for a party, etc.?

My research on approaches to become more persistent turned up several examples, including Lou Macabasco's, *6 Effective Ways to Become Persistent* on LifeHack.com. As the title indicates, the reader is provided with a simple breakdown of steps to become more persistent. The benefits of becoming a more persistent person certainly outweigh any negative consequences. Anyone who knows me, knows this, as I practice being focused and persistent every day.

A long-time and close friend of mine, Carol Agranat, is a professional coach at Career Mapping Solutions. I guarantee you she works with all her clients on first developing an end game, or goal. In my opinion, the most interesting part of Carol's job is that she works with people who span the entire spectrum — from recent college grads to mid-career professionals, as well as people who want to switch occupations or re-enter the work force. The common thread for all of her clients is their desire to move onto the next level of their career, a pursuit that will require persistence.

Although I have not confirmed this, I can imagine the most satisfying part of Carol's job is helping people create a pathway towards their professional goals, and seeing them be achieved. Having been a lacrosse player and lacrosse coach for a number of years, as well as a certified motivational coach for executives as well as people at various stages of their career, there is almost nothing more gratifying in helping someone else or a team achieve what they may not have thought was possible.

One of my secrets to help people to achieve what they set out to, is to encourage them to believe they can accomplish their goal or goals. By breaking down the steps to reach the finish line, similar to the steps outlined in Macabasco's book, I've seen that achieving any goal is entirely possible.

If you do not believe in yourself, find someone who does! There's a song from the musical, *How to Succeed in Business Without Really Trying* called "I Believe In You!" Check it out.

*This story is dedicated to Carol Agranat, whom I have known for than 30 years, and who is one of the most courageous, genuinely passionate people about helping others to succeed. Thank you for your friendship, Carol, and may you continue to do amazing work with others.*

## Is Fear Driving Your Decisions?

*Whether you are aware of it or not, fear might drive more of your decisions than you realize. But what if your decisions were not driven by fear, but instead by a renewed sense of confidence in knowing you can rely upon your gut instincts to provide the right decision with a far more positive outcome?*

All of us make continuous decisions, but have you stopped to think about whether they are based on being completely confident, or are your decisions fear-based due to a lack of confidence? Trusting your gut is something most people, in general, have a hard time doing.

Why? Because we are so conditioned to seek others' opinions, acceptance, and approval, we often make decisions based on how they will be perceived. This is fear-based decision making.

Many work-based scenarios involve coming to a consensus. This is often when the ultimate decision agreed upon is less likely to be based on what would be the best decision. The result is that the decision was likely influenced by fear. When a consensus is required, people generally resort to projecting in their minds what they think others will want the decision to be, and not what it should be if fear were not part of the equation. So how do you stop making decisions being based on fear?

I often have conversations with business people about the concept of listening to the voice of reason in their brain. Think of there being two voices in your head — one of them is a positive influence, the other negative. The positive is your natural instinct, which offers sound and reasonable guidance, while the other voice is fear. It is not based on any type of instinct.

The challenge is to practice silencing the negative voice. You can start doing this with less complicated decisions such as thinking through a typical scenario everyone deals with — working late. Think about your response to the decision about whether to stay a bit later at work to finish a project. If you listened to your positive, gut instinct, it would likely confirm that it is okay to spend slightly more time at work to complete a project. As a result, you will not be stressed all night at home about the project not being completed on time or advanced to a point of comfort.

This decision illustrates not being afraid to commit some additional work hours in order to have more time to relax, stress free, later.

If, however, you decided not to stay, your negative voice was probably presenting fear-based reasons why you should not — you don't have the energy, you should have planned your time better, you will be missing out on so many other things later that night, etc.

Another way to understand why fear plays a role in our decision making is to actually think about what fear means. Thanks to numerous citations, I do not know who to credit the representation of fear as F.E.A.R., a memorable acronym for False Evidence Appearing Real. This nicely supports the negative voice concept. Indeed, most of the time, if I stop to think when making a decision, I remind myself of this simple acronym.

Do you make decisions based on fear?

Most people will admit some portion of their decisions are based on relying upon their gut or the positive voice, but far too many make a large amount of their decisions based on fear. The first and best step to take to stop making fear-based decisions is to recognize and admit to doing so.

Once you've done that, start to consciously make and think through your decisions based on your initial gut decision, and to then go with it.

Over time, review the decisions you have made with your gut, and see how often these are the best and strongest. Once you start relying on your gut or positive voice, you will approach making decisions in an entirely different manner. You will also feel a new sense of freedom of not second guessing or making decisions once made primarily from a position of fear.

## The Failure of Not Following Up

*Having strong follow-up skills is a discipline. Just like adding reps to your workout, building follow-up skills requires practice to net results. Following up is not simply for sales or marketing people, it is a skill that, when mastered and done consistently, will reap enormously positive results. How would you rate your ability to follow-up on any item you have committed to doing?*

Promises, promises: "My word is my bond." A simple, unattributed phrase used for centuries to indicate that one will always do what one has promised. I could chose a number of different words to express my sentiments about most people's ability to follow-up on just about anything, but in my experience, most fail miserably, and yes, I will say the word … simply *stink* at it.

Why is it that something that is so simple to do is simply skipped (or ignored) by the majority of people in the business community, and in many social interaction scenarios as well?

Is it because they were not taught this skill, or lack manners or discipline? Is it because they forget what they promised to follow-up on, or did they not ever intend to follow up and simply gave lip service and told someone what they think they wanted to hear?

Effective follow-up skills are not innate, they are learned. No matter how stellar your communication skills, mastering the art of follow up requires discipline. Unless you've spent time studying this specific niche of communication before, your skills probably need some work.

When I encounter someone who has strong follow-up skills, I am always impressed. The people who consistently do this well are not always in sales, customer service, or marketing — business disciplines with excellent follow-through skills. But they do share a common thread: They are highly self-disciplined, driven to succeed, value the reputation of their verbal promises, and have genuine respect for the person to whom they committed.

Think how you feel when someone follows up with you: Are you surprised, or did you expect this to happen? Did their follow through seem like a large effort, or did it potentially take less than a couple of moments to accomplish?

Let's think about follow-up from a different angle. When someone does not follow through with a commitment, does it change your opinion of them? And have you ever considered how you are perceived when you failed to follow through? Do you think there was a negative impact on your lack of follow-up?

When I was researching this topic, I wondered when and how people learn the art of following through. In most academic situations, an early form of practicing this skill is to complete and turn in your homework, and there is an incentive to do so. But follow through is not a skill taught in school. Unless you learn this commitment from family, friends, or colleagues, you may not be fully equipped to master this skill until you are put into scenarios which require you to do so.

Being able to follow through on your commitments is a relatively easy skill to master, and includes a change in attitude to care about the importance of this skill.

Here's a challenge to consider trying for one week. See what happens after you commit to following through on everything you told someone you would do. Keep track of the results, then look back on the results and think about the impact this exercise has had on you and the recipients. Was it as difficult or time consuming as you imagined it to be?

The benefits to following through will be how people perceive you in a much more positive light. Your personal reputation will gain what I refer to as "Karma points" — an added bonus of simply doing the right thing!

So, what is the first thing you are going to follow-up on?

## The Commonality of Dogs and Meetings

*I am fairly sure you would agree you like dogs better than meetings, even if you are not an animal lover. Puppies vs Meetings — no contest. Puppies win every time! Most people dread meetings, and I used to as well, before I learned the secrets of how to have amazing, productive, and short gatherings that garner results.*

We have all been there. You were probably in one today. You know, that dreaded meeting you had to attend although you felt like sucked the life right out of you. I'm sure at some point you asked yourself, "Do I really need to be here," or, "Is this a good use of my time," or, "Will this meeting ever end?"

If you did, I guarantee it's because either you, or the person who arranged the session, does not know how to make meetings a useful part of any day. I remember what they were like before I learned the secret to having a fun meeting. I distinctly recall an email from HR suggesting I take a two-day course on how to have useful and meaningful meetings. At first I thought this was actually a practical joke, but when I read through the agenda, it piqued my curiosity. This may sound ridiculous, but this two-day internal course on how to have productive meetings ranks among the top five things I have learned as a business executive.

Let's review the basic elements of planning and facilitating a productive meeting. But first, a word of caution. Prepare to be committed to following these principles, and know that doing so is an addictive process (but not one for which you will need any rehab.) Here are five guidelines to embrace in order to love your future meetings as much as you adore puppies.

1. Define the purpose and goal of the meeting. If you can't, then you do not need to have a meeting.

2. Develop an agenda, including the amount of time you will spend on each item. Also include any pre-work that needs to be accomplished, such as reviewing a document, talking to co-workers or team members to gain consensus, doing research on the topic, and so on.

3. Determine who needs to be invited, and what role they will play in the meeting. Tag them as speaker, participant, guest expert, note-taker, etc.

4. Send the meeting notice early enough to provide recipients with enough time to complete any pre-work. Schedule it at a time that works with the majority of your colleagues' schedules.

5. Stick to the agenda, and take notes during the meeting. Share the meeting notes. Be sure to identify who has action items and an agreed-upon timeline for each to be accomplished. Include contact information as a further time-saver.

Most meetings do not need to be longer than 30 minutes. Most people lose interest and focus after a half hour. With practice and planning, you can even reduce your meeting time to what I call "micro meetings" of 15 minutes or less. Imagine that! Micro meetings are my favorite. They are similar to what the software and other industries call a "scrum" meeting method.* Both are hyper-productive.

Fast forward a month from now, and see if having productive meetings has changed your outlook and attendance. I know it was a stretch to ask you to imagine what puppies and meetings have in common, but I know if you embrace the concepts outlined above, you will see the common factor is that you will like both puppies and meetings. Side benefit? Consider how much time you will get back on your calendar.

Your challenge is to become a master of the micro meeting, and to share your secrets with others. They will thank you for doing so — but hopefully not by licking your hand.

*The daily Scrum is a brief meeting, ideally held at the start of each day, by companies who follow Agile Methodology that offers iterative and incremental decision-making and project management. Every team member who works towards the completion of a given sprint must participate. All team members should attend and stand during the meeting. The daily Scrum meeting should ideally not last more than 15 minutes, because nobody wants to stand for more than 15 minutes.

# Be More Decisive!

*Not everyone feels comfortable with making a decision; but being decisive and trusting your instincts about your decision will prove to become a valuable business tool for you if you do this well.*

Making a decision seems to be a process that is increasingly becoming more difficult in both professional environments, and at home. I have noticed a trend in people deferring decisions, or what I will call "over consulting" with others.

Having the Internet at our fingertips has contributed towards this trend, allowing everyone to easily, yet unnecessarily, over research and over analyze situations. There's a saying I heard recently: "When you analyze, you paralyze." Is this you?

When I speak to others about how they make decisions, the majority tell me they find it difficult. Why is this the case, and what are the benefits to delaying, or simply not being decisive?

Having worked in the business world for more than 20 years, I acknowledge that my decision-making abilities have matured and accelerated over the years. In the past, I relied upon trusted advisors or mentors to help me apply their wider and more polished perspective to each situation. I highly recommend, especially to those just starting out, to surround yourself with people you can rely upon for advice and counsel — formal or informal mentors who can help you make decisions, but not insist one way or the other.

My experience in having made thousands of decisions during my career and gaining more confidence with each one has contributed to my ability to make decisions more quickly. My experience has also allowed me to apply more layers of considerations factored into decisions, arguably making them much sounder, stronger, and defensible.

There a variety of decision category types, but for the purposes of this article, let's focus on making decisions in a business environment. When employees are empowered to make decisions on their own, and not by a committee, I have found they are more satisfied in their roles.

They also are more decisive, and take better and more calculated risks, or what some refer to as "fail fast" decisions. But many of these quick, definitive decisions produce extraordinary results, and the employee and employer both gain the benefit of time being on their side. When decisions are elongated, and mulled over either by an individual or a committee, they lose the benefit of what could have produced positive results right away. Yes, the opposite is possible, but based on another article in this book — "The Impact of Positive Thinking" on pages 75-76 — consider how you can accelerate your decisions.

Switching gears and focusing on you, now think about some of the times when you have been in a situation when you have been waiting for a decision to be made, or had to make a decision. Waiting can feel like an eternity. Conversely, when you are the one making a decision, you may feel actual physical pressure as your body tightens as the minutes tick by.

My friends who are yoga and meditation experts would tell you to take deep breaths and slow your thinking. This is good advice regardless of the situation, but wouldn't you agree you feel better and more satisfied when you make a decision? Granted you might not be 100% satisfied, but in my experience, it sure beats being indecisive. Yes, I will also agree not making a decision is a decision, but in my professional experience, it is better to make a definitive decision.

Need a little more advice on making decisions? Check out "11 Genius Tips to Be More Decisive" in *Success Magazine*, for more tips.

We will all be better off if people we work with make an effort to be more decisive, and yes, make a decision and not vacillate, delay, or opt not to decide.

Please consider being more decisive. I promise you others will appreciate you doing so. Give it a try and see what happens. And if you cannot do this well on your own, please make a decision to find a mentor or advisor to help!

## How to Amp Up Your Swagger

*You are extraordinary, but you may not know it, or you may not show it. Amplify your swagger and have others start to notice how fabulous you really are. Here are some ways to increase your swagger, starting today.*

Swagger. What is it, and how do you get some? Mick Jagger oozes swagger. Dwayne "The Rock" Johnson has plenty, too. Tina Turner and Beyoncé — oh, my!

All certainly seem to be having more fun, or at least more outward success than others. Perhaps it is all an illusion, or only perceived by some and not others. My take on the definition of swagger is a bit different. Over the years, I have heard it used more as an adjective to define someone who exudes confidence and has an air of charisma or electricity about them that sets them apart from others.

Assuming it is possible to obtain more swagger, how does one go about doing so? Perhaps you could begin with your attire. Consider the fact celebrities rely upon professional stylists to select their often outrageous, always attention-getting, outfits. They do this for numerous reasons, but mainly to ensure they control their vision of how they want to be perceived by the public.

The psychology behind fashion and how and why people choose their clothing is a topic that could be explored on its own, but think of the last time you wore a new outfit. Did you feel different, better, or more attractive? Did you stand taller; were your shoulders back? Did you feel more confident, or even eager to talk to people you might not otherwise seek out had you been wearing one of the items you've had in your closet for a while?

Are you dressing for the job you want, or the job you have?

Hairstyles can come into play for both sexes and amp-up your swagger quotient, providing it's the right cut and color. (Hint: Extreme hair cuts or colors might not be adding to your swagger, but in fact detracting from it). Most people notice when others get their hair styled, and typically will comment in a positive way, although not always.

Having the right hairstyle can make you look younger, older, even more fashionable. I don't know about you, but I can never achieve the same look the stylist does, that's why we go to them in the first place! I consider myself hair challenged from a styling perspective, and I am going out on a limb by assuming most people place themselves in this category as well.

Becoming proficient at something can contribute to increasing your confidence and swagger, too. It does not matter what it is you are good at, I simply encourage you to do more of whatever it is you find you are doing that delivers a positive result. Perhaps you are an accomplished gourmet cook, you help others who need assistance, you can draw realistic images of anything, or you have mastered the art of hosting amazing parties. (Refer to page 3 to read how to make these part of your Value Proposition.)

Everyone is good at one thing; some people are good at many things. If you do not know your strengths, ask your friends and family to help you sort this out. Or check out the book *Strengths Finders 2.0* by Tom Rath, and take the on-line survey that will reveal your top five. Mine are Positivity, Strategic, Arranger, Individualization, and Woo, which means "Winning Others Over." There are 34 possible strengths, and it's really fun to find out what yours are.

Add more swagger to your life and see if people take notice. Make a mental note if you feel differently by focusing on doing things that help you set yourself apart from others.

As I tell my children all the time, being ordinary is not an option when you can be extraordinary.

## Navigating to the Next Level

*Depending on where you are in your career, chances are you have thought about how to get to the next level in your company, or perhaps another firm. Consider yourself fortunate if you work at a company that has developed career paths for you to follow. The majority of people who work at small to mid-size companies do not typically have this same advantage. Either way, why not develop your own career path?*

At some point in their career, most people have thought about what it would take to move to the next level. Most firms with more than 100 employees generally have developed a career path for you to consider; start-ups, or rapidly growing organizations, however, may not have had time to do this. So, without a defined career path already in place, how does one navigate to the next level?

Assume you are ready to advance your career within the next three to six months. Knowing the rules of engagement when it comes to navigating to the next level will save you time and energy.

This may seem counterintuitive, but you need to first think about why you want to move up the ladder. Is it because you have been in the role for more than 12-18 months and have plateaued in terms of your learning curve? Are you eager and ready for more responsibility and a pay raise? Or, are you thinking it is time to move to the next level simply because you see your peers in the company or at similar organizations making upward career moves?

Some companies have a defined a policy on career advancement that requires an employee work in their current role for a set amount of time before they can be considered for a promotion. So, check your company's handbook or ask the HR department. That way, you won't be disappointed to find out you will not be able to move into a new role for a period of time.

Most companies offer an annual performance review. This is the perfect time to talk to your boss about your career path options within the company. If your company does not offer an annual review, you can ask your boss to provide you with one, or ask your HR department if they could assist you in this process. Prior to your review, chronicle all of your accomplishments in the past year, and be able to provide examples of how they have contributed to helping the company.

Next, think about how you would be able to take on more responsibility. Explore ways to become an even more productive employee and advance in your current role through on-line classes, industry-related events, or networking events. Networking opportunities offer a chance to talk to others who are in roles above you, and to learn what they did to move up to the next level. The majority of people you talk to will be happy to share how they navigated their career advancements. What you will quickly find is that there are multiple ways to do so.

Be sure to leverage others' advice as you plot your upward mobility strategy. Climbing the career ladder is really a team exercise — even though it may not appear to be one.

Before you begin your journey toward career advancement, seek and secure a mentor who can figuratively walk beside you through the process. A mentor should be someone who has what you want — a particular position, superior ethics, enthusiasm, a gift for gab . . . decide what you're lacking and hook yourself to a winner.

Your mentor can either be someone within the company at a more senior level, or someone from outside. He or she will be able to help you to think through and plot out a strategy for your career advancement. A mentor can also candidly let you know whether they think you are ready to move to the next career level, as you may not have the insight and experience required to know whether you are ready to climb the ladder by leaps and bounds, or one step at a time.

Navigating to the next career level can be simultaneously exciting and nerve wracking. Using the energy from being eager to explore moving up takes practice, so keep this in mind as you are going through the process.

# Chapter 2 | Work/Life

## Reputation

*Your professional reputation can take years to successfully cultivate, but just one mistake to sink. Maneuvering professionally is equivalent to navigating a land mine a day at a time. What are some of the things you can do to avoid stepping on a professional land mine, and to mitigate the damage done to your reputation should you bomb?*

Building your professional reputation is something you have been doing one day at a time since you joined the workforce. You have also built your reputation one company at a time, one team at a time, and perhaps one project at a time, too. In other words, every company, every person with whom you work, and the projects to which you have contributed are all part of what combines to define your professional reputation.

How you handle yourself in each and every encounter is also a contributing factor that either adds to or subtracts from the value of your reputation. So, what happens if you have built a solid and positive reputation and you do or say something that has a negative impact? Is it possible to recover?

The answer is yes and no; time, in many cases can work in your favor. Why? Because most people are more focused on themselves than you, and not everyone will remember all of the details of the incident in question.

It's probably easy to name several people who have fallen prey to being victims either by self sabotage or because of a  person or group who negatively impacted the perceptions of others. This is one reason people or companies hire public relations or crisis management firms to help mitigate the damage done to a brand due to a negative incident. Tylenol,

Perrier, Exxon and other companies all had major incidents which severely tarnished the brand. Both time and redrafting their messaging helped restore the brand, or took them out of the harsh spotlight of scrutiny.

Now think about people who have seen their reputation tarnished. It is painful to watch, and even more traumatic to experience. People find out who their true friends and supporters are in these cases. Those who faired best when their reputation took a turn downwards were the ones who had high degrees of emotional intelligence, but more importantly, surrounded themselves with a support network to help to rebuild their personal brand.

Of course, we are all responsible of our own reputations, but having a strong professional support group, can work miracles. This is possible because the supporter essentially acts as a reputation buffer when the crash occurs. Having these human "airbags" takes serious quality time to build; however, once they are in place, unless the incident was completely egregious or ethically challenging, most people will be able to play a support role in restoring someone else's professional reputation.

Since social media can build or break a career, reputations need to be simultaneously guarded, but also nurtured. The speed at which this communication channel moves makes it both positive and negative in terms of having an impact on your professional reputation. There are safeguards to control some of the negative aspects of social media, but more importantly, the positive attributes should be optimized. It's okay to toot your own horn once in a while — perhaps you won an award, earned a certification, made a significant contribution to a business project, or volunteered time to a worthy cause. Take a bow, and build your reputation.

Although no one wants to have an incident impact their professional reputation, it can happen. Although the immediate aftermath feels devastating, you can recover. Do not to let it define who you are. Most people are good by nature, and there are more who will forget what you did than remember what happened, or when. Keep your chin up, do the right thing when faced with tough choices, and most importantly, do what you can to preserve your reputation when you have an opportunity.

## The Value of Staying in Touch

*People have good intentions of remaining in touch with one another, but for some reason, most people do not make it a priority. The benefits of keeping in touch with family, friends, and business associates is immeasurable, and far outweigh the effort it takes. It can take years to develop relationships, so why wouldn't you want to nurture these precious connections?*

A wise friend recently told me he was impressed with my ability to keep in touch. In full disclosure, I had lost touch with this person for a number of years; but when we reconnected, it felt like we had picked right back up on our last conversation from too many years ago to mention. Since re-establishing our friendship, both of us have benefitted from the life and professional experience we have each gained. Better yet, he has been true to his word to help me on a request I made in a recent email exchange. The original intent of reconnecting took an entirely different turn than I expected it to, but therein lies the beauty of staying in touch.

Perhaps my communications background gives me an advantage over most people, or perhaps because I genuinely like to stay connected. I also think I am driven to remain in contact with people because of the value they bring to enriching my life.

In his book, *Never Eat Alone*, author Keith Ferrazzi explains how he fulfills the value of staying in touch with his network by making sure he leverages every dining opportunity he can. Ferrazzi writes he also reaches out to new people and dines with them to develop a connection. It's a concept I try to put it into practice myself. It does take a fair amount of effort, but it is absolutely worth doing.

Another tip from Ferrazzi is to maximize travel time. He uses free moments on the train or plane to either leave voice mails for people he's been out of touch with, or schedules time to catch up on the phone if distance prohibits them from connecting in person.

With vast technological improvements in our ability and ease of being able to keep in touch through voice, video, text, or social media, there are no excuses for not increasing our outreach. Facebook offers a way to find a distant cousin with whom we've lost track. How fun! But if you've let serious time lag between business connections, you're missing out on potential opportunities. Someone may want to reconnect with you, but misplaced your contact information or forgot your last name.

And when's the last time you updated your LinkedIn profile? You never know who will send you a money-making message.

Just as with an exercise routine, the more you work on your ability to stay in touch, the easier it becomes to do. Schedule social media time right into your calendar — at least an hour a week — no need to overdo it. Send a note to someone with whom you've worked or done business with before — who knows where that will lead? And make the time to send a hand-written note or a simple Thinking of You greeting card.

My father, who purchased his first iPhone at age 75, has already mastered the art of smart phone technology. He uses it to keep in touch with his children and seven grandkids, to whom he texts, sends photos, emojis, and links to daily. Dad's iPhone has significantly increased his ability to remain in touch with our family, as well as his friends. I know he would agree he would not be as connected to others without it.

Everyone should be able to do this. Remaining in touch has never been easier to do, so stop procrastinating and start reaching out to people you have lost touch with, have not spoken to in a while (define for yourself what this means), or take a more strategic approach and make a list of people you want to reconnect with and begin re-establishing contact with them this week.

Given all the stress over current events worldwide, why not turn your communication outreaches into positive experiences from which you and the recipient will both benefit. As Nike says, Just Do It©.

The ROI is phenomenal.

## How to Talk to *Anyone*

*Have you ever wondered why it seems effortless for some people to be able to talk to almost anyone, anytime, or anywhere? With technological gadgets seemingly taking over our lives each day, the art of face-to-face conversation is something fewer people, especially the millennial generation, are adept at, much less practicing regularly.*

What if you knew about a simple technique that would allow you to easily have a conversation with *anyone* you desired — wouldn't you want to know about it? Would it help you personally or professionally? Of course it would!

About 25 years ago while we were having lunch at work, a good friend asked me what I thought was a very simple, yet deep, question. She asked me how I could so easily have conversations with everyone I encountered. I realized perhaps starting up a conversation with a stranger didn't come easily for others. I took for granted my ability to talk with others so easily. What had I done differently in my life to make chatting with others happen so naturally? My answer might surprise you!

I have always found it easy to talk to other people because I am genuinely interested, truly curious to learn more about them. The only way I know how to learn more about other people is to ask them questions, and not be afraid to do so.

Typically, I will ask an open-ended question, that doesn't permit a *yes* or *no* answer. This allows me to naturally ask follow-up questions. When I began explaining my approach to my friend, I told her what now, looking back, is one of the greatest and easiest things to teach someone. All you need to do is to have a few simple questions you can ask that will get the other person talking.

For example, begin by asking someone if they have any travel plans, or have recently been somewhere they would recommend to others, such as a vacation, business trip, or personal experience — something different than their daily routine, and that they'd be willing to talk about (e.g., white water rafting). People love talking about themselves, even if they are shy. By asking them an open-ended question, you allow them to feel comfortable with the conversation, which then allows them to ask additional questions. This exchange can often lead to fascinating information you would not otherwise have discovered.

Having enjoyed thousands of conversations in my lifetime, what I am most surprised by, and I think you will be, too, is how once you get someone talking, you will be amazed at how infrequently they will reciprocate and ask you questions back. People who are skilled at conversing will ask you questions — and more than a few of them. But many will not, and this is a shame because the more you chat with others, the more skilled you become as a conversationalist. This enhanced skill can ultimately lead to a lifetime of opportunities you would not otherwise have if you did not begin the conversation in the first place.

By interacting with others, you are planting the seeds of developing a relationship, and allowing them to more easily talk with you again. By asking questions, they will also be more inclined to like you as a person; and let's face it, I am always telling people you can never have too many friends.

If you have not had a conversation with a stranger or someone you only slightly know, give this technique a try. You will be delighted at the possibilities of where the conversation can or will take you. If nothing else, you will have practiced the art of active listening and response that we all should master.

## It's All About Now

*We live in a time when people seem to have lost the ability to be patient. Instant gratification can be thrilling and sometimes even rewarding, but not everything needs to be done right now. What is the downside to the power of now?*

I'll admit that patience is probably not one of my super powers. To my credit, I do practice being patient, and many people who have worked with me actually think I *am* patient.

Perhaps I come across as patient, but if I were a duck, you would likely see my feet paddling extremely fast underneath the calm surface of the water. Appearing to be patient can have advantages, though. In many business situations, it is imperative to come across as steady, yet able to make swift and well thought-out decisions when necessary.

There have been numerous articles written about the power of now, and a book with that very title by Eckhart Tolle extols the virtues of spiritual enlightenment, living in the moment, and not concerning yourself with thoughts from the past.

In the business world, we are trained to look in our rearview mirror and to leverage this information to inform our decisions. This knowledge will make us more competitive. When we take the time to slow down and leverage analysis to help with strategic planning, we go against the concept of instant gratification. But this is absolutely required and usually takes years of experience to do well.

Being strategic about decisions can be a challenge, especially if you're a newcomer to the business world. It can also be frustrating to those who are driven by our instant gratification society.

We are fortunate to have technology to rely upon to help provide insights into data that even five years ago would have been difficult to obtain or analyze. Reading and interpreting the numbers is a skill best developed over time. Having instant access can be enormously beneficial, but taking the time to review the information with more experienced peers will serve you well.

An example of this would be reviewing your social media marketing investments to determine if they are providing you with the expected results you desire or forecasted. Fortunately social media is one of the marketing investment areas which can be adjusted in "real time" if the results are not suitable, and this is one example of appealing to instant gratification.

Not all business disciplines are driven by instant gratification, but sales and marketing teams often are. This is fueled by expectations from senior management who either report to a board of directors or potentially to venture capitalists who have extremely high expectations. In both of these instances, time is not on the side of the teams who are on the front lines of performance. There is a great deal of pressure on these teams to perform well, and in the spirit of now.

Depending on how the powers that be manage their teams, employees working for them will be captured by a great sense of urgency and potentially a feeling of being under a performance microscope. It is critical that upper management know how to minimize these emotions, as this type of pressure is not sustainable.

Seasoned managers know how to guide their teams through bursts of pressure and show them how to embrace the power of instant gratification in smaller doses. Since marketing and sales teams are typically quarterly driven, they should pace themselves through their performance journeys.

Some people are naturally adept at pacing themselves, but most people need a bit of guidance or coaching, and over sustained periods of time. Having superior time management skills will contribute to making the marathon pace seem less daunting, and allow the team to embrace the concept of slowing down enough to realize they do not need to have instant gratification for every aspect of their work.

# Mastering the Art of Interpreting Body Language

*Reading body language can be learned, but for some people, it is a natural interpretive instinct. I have seen numerous instances of people who do not know how to interpret body language, and who are simultaneously unaware of how theirs is conveying how they really feel to others. Understanding how to read body language is an essential business skill. Have you mastered it yet?*

Understanding how to interpret body language, or how a cocked head, a glance at your watch, or an inadvertent eye roll speak volumes about how you feel, is an essential business skill. Unfortunately, educators in the U.S. do not teach reading and interpreting body language in business or any other school. So, how does someone learn how to do this?

The simple answer is to educate yourself. I found an Internet site that provided a helpful general overview of how to interpret most signals. Check out a few and see which ones speak to you.

Talking to others and learning from their experience is another approach. Paying more attention during future interactions with your family, friends, and colleagues will help you to practice and become more skilled at interpreting the body clues you're sending and receiving.

To understand how you come across to others, I recommend asking people you are comfortable with for feedback. Remind them of a few instances they have observed your body language in either happy, neutral, or contentious situations. And if they have not yet watched you, unguarded, what a wonderful opportunity for both you and they to learn or practice!

Another option is to pay closer attention to your own physical reactions during conversational engagements. For example, do you cross your arms when you do not like what you are hearing; do you look down at the floor when you feel threatened; or does your laugh sound different when you are nervous?

I recently observed a colleague's body language — he was totally unaware of my experiment. Sitting across from two of my colleagues, it became apparent to me one of them was unaware of how to read body language, and did not understand the messages his body was conveying to the person with whom we were talking.

Without giving any corporate secrets away, the conversation was between the head of marketing ("Marketing"), and the head of sales ("Sales"). During the conversation, Marketing offered to have his team take on some work — and Sales would be the beneficiary.

The sales team had been asking for this work to be done for months. However, during this interaction, Sales began to fold his arms over his chest. Folded arms essentially mean the person was either not listening, did not believe, was uncomfortable with the conversation, or was rejecting what was being said.

This was the opposite reaction I expected. After the meeting, I asked Sales if he was happy about the offer made by the marketing team. He said he was happy with what he heard. What he did not realize, however, was that his body language expressed the opposite of this emotion.

Wonder what I'll be working on next? If you guessed teaching a client about body language, you'd get an A+.

## Become More Confident

*Why do some people have more confidence than others? Is it possible to increase your self-confidence? Yes, if desired, you can build and maintain confidence.*

Where does self-confidence come from? Are some people born with more than others, or is it a skill or strength developed over time? I am sure you have encountered people who seem to have a level of confidence way beyond their chronological age. Still, there are others who are at a point in their lives and careers where they should have a high degree of self-reliance, yet are severely lacking it, and for no apparent reason.

There are numerous ways to increase your self-confidence. A simple Google search will produce links galore, including one that compiled 25 simple actions to boost your self-confidence, all of which are completely easy to achieve.

As I read through the list, I mentally ticked off the boxes to determine if they were achievable. In case you think only non-celebrities suffer from lack of self-confidence, my research revealed numerous successful people who seemingly reached the pinnacle of their careers or talent, yet were plagued with lack of confidence. Examples include singers Mariah Carey and the late David Bowie; tennis superstar Serena Williams; and Academy, Golden Globes, and Grammy award-winning actress Kate Winslet.

Each of these celebrities have documented a history of battling low self-esteem. How is it possible for these superstars in their respective fields to not have over-the-top levels of confidence? Part of the reason has to do with the negative narratives they have running in their minds, which has them perceive themselves far differently than the outside world does. Another contributing factor to low or lack of self-confidence is not believing in yourself, even though there is vast evidence to the contrary that you should be able to do so.

Building self-confidence is not something you can do overnight, but *is* something you can work on every day. The methods to building self-confidence need to be practiced daily, and yes, you will have days when your confidence is lower or higher. The goal is to maintain a balance in your level of self-confidence. This can be done, like most everything else, with constant practice.

A quick way to increase self-confidence is to stand in front of a mirror, put your hands on your hips and pose like Superman or Wonder Woman. Now, tell your new image, out loud and proud, "I've got this!" five or six times or until you feel a positive change in your demeanor. You will be amazed at how such a simple action can make you feel more confident than you were just a few minutes earlier. I have leveraged this technique numerous times. Give it a try.

*This article is dedicated to my daughter, Bronwyn Shinnick, the most confident person I know. Bronwyn also inspires me daily with her drive to succeed and her magnificent level of focus and confidence.*

## Developing Your Professional Network

*Developing your professional network takes time and effort. It can also be tremendously fun to do. What's more, the relationships you develop will help in ways beyond how you might imagine.*

There's a saying we've all heard: "It's not *what* you know, it's *who* you know."

When I first heard this expression, it annoyed me, and for many years, I did not want to give it much merit. But as my career developed, I realized it might have more strength as a concept than I gave it credit.

When you think about your network and the people with whom you regularly engage, have you considered whether you have consciously developed your network, or has it developed organically from the people you have met?

In his book, *Never Eat Alone*, author Keith Ferrazzi advises us to take every opportunity to network, especially during dining opportunities. His "never dine alone" strategy is particularly appropriate when traveling to a convention. Just invite yourself to a table and begin chatting. Start with weather, which is always a safe topic. Who knows who you'll meet or where a chance encounter could lead? Ferrazzi believes that whether you realize it or not, your expanded network will afford you opportunities for career advancement or moves into industries in which you may not have foundational experience.

As an executive coach and professional sports and business performance advisor, I routinely talk to clients about the importance of growing their network, when they step out of their comfort zone and meet new people. For those who dread the thought, I suggest they start with their current network. It is far less intimidating to approach a person with whom you already have something in common.

Developing your network does not always have to be accomplished in person, but when possible, this would be my recommendation. The second-best way to meet new connections is by scheduling a 10-15-minute call. Develop two or three bullet points prior to the call, share the list with them, and then stick to the script to respect their time and honor your own. If the conversation is going well, you can always schedule additional time, or agree to meet in person, if this is possible.

If you have the opportunity to travel, schedule brief, in-person meetings with members of your current network, and with one or two other people you'd like to meet.

It is critical to make sure you are always actively engaged with your current network, as the more time you invest, the larger the dividend may be — often when you least expect it.

Another factor to remember about networking is that it is, or should be, a two-way street. Always ask the person with whom you are networking what you can do for them, and to sincerely offer to help them in some way. It could be offering to talk to either someone they know who would like advice, or perhaps extending them an opportunity to be connected to someone in your network. You may not be able to reciprocate immediately, but let them know you'll be on the lookout for opportunities. Or perhaps you're the one on the receiving end? If so, just say thank you. A handwritten follow-up note would be a feather in your cap.

Meeting new people is one of the most exciting things I routinely look forward to doing. I am one of those people who look at strangers as simply people I have not had the opportunity to meet and get to know yet. Over the years, this attitude has served me extremely well. I do not overtly work on developing my network, but instead look for informal opportunities to do so, in places I am going to, or when I will be in social settings when I do not know everyone at the event. By not placing too much emphasis on whether I am growing my network, it more organically tends to develop, and which I think is a good model for others to follow.

The most important thing to remember about networking is to have fun with the process. Too many people stress themselves out by thinking they constantly need to be networking. They do not, and I do not recommend doing so.

*My parents have served as great examples for me about the importance of cultivating my network, or what I refer to as my professional friends. This article is dedicated to my Father, Daniel I. Murphy.*

## Finding Your Purpose

*Have you considered aligning your career with what fuels your innate purpose or passion? Think of how amazing going to work each day would be if we could all do this.*

How often do you ask yourself, why am I doing this? This could be a reference to your work, leisure activities, relationship, or (fill-in-the-blank). For the sake of narrowing the scope, let's focus on work, as we all spend countless hours devoted to our occupations. Unless you won the lottery, have a trust fund, or have figured out a way to have a stream of income with little effort applied, you will likely be working most of your life.

What if you woke up each morning and had a job or career that gave you a sense of purpose?

One of my favorite books is *Strengths Finder 2.0* by Tom Rath. A close second is *Destination Unstoppable* by Maureen Electa Monte. Monte's book helped me focus and crystalize a professional purpose towards which I have been driving — to make other people see and capitalize on their strengths. When you are able to focus and make the most of your strengths, everything starts to align both professionally and personally, and you can more clearly see your purpose in life.

Working with sales and marketing teams my entire career, it's ironic that I did not realize one of my strengths was something that allowed me to see in others strengths they may not have seen in themselves. That particular strength is what *Strengths Finder* refers to as "Individualization." In essence, this means I see each person as a snowflake with all the special, significant characteristics that make them so unique.

Having this ability is something I readily share with others. It has allowed me to help them see the potential they have in themselves. When individuals understand and focus on their potential, magical things begin to happen. They discover a renewed sense of joy and purpose doing what they are spending their career time on.

A true story from the pages of *Destination Unstoppable* chronicles how a midwestern prep school hockey team came together as an unbeatable force in a short period of time — right at the end of their season, which helped the squad to (Spoiler Alert) win the state championship. There were a number of factors that contributed towards the team uniting for victory. But ultimately, each player was focused on having his own strengths contribute to the team daily, on and off the ice. Imagine if you could be focused on applying your unique strengths to your career!

Let's assume you are not in a job that fires your passion and fuels your purpose. Have you considered either seeking another role within the company, or researching firms or organizations that are selling products or services in stronger alignment with your passion?

This advice is commonly given to people either early in their career, or considered when you have been in an unsatisfying career choice for a period of time. Regardless of what you may be thinking, please keep in mind you are never "stuck."

If you are spending valuable time working in a job or career that is not fueling your desire to be purposeful, consider changing this situation. Yes, you have the power to do this. Ask others for help if you do not know where to begin, but please get started on finding your career purpose. It's out there for you to discover. Now go find it.

This trope is true – when you find a job you love, you'll never work another day.

## How to Hire Persistent Optimists

*Persistence might be one of the most important business super powers one can possess. Most people have some percentage of this ability. How they leverage the power to be persistent, can produce amazing results. Find supporters who can enhance your persistence super power. Learn to identify and then surround yourself with these critical supporters, and watch magic happen.*

Being persistent can produce amazing results, but it also takes dedication and patience. Warning: It will not be an overnight magic show. Persistence takes time and patience, but it is one of the greatest traits a business person can possess.

Some professions require greater amounts of persistence to obtain the experience or education to reach the top level in their field. Most people generally feel satisfied when they reach their goal. What they all have in common is their internal drive or persistence.

Is being persistent an inherent trait, or can it be learned, perhaps by modeling the behavior of others? Of course, there are varying degrees of persistence, but the most common level is one that allows a person to remain hyper-focused on reaching their goal.

So how does one go about staying focused?

Some people who have trouble getting focused rely on medication for help. Others have used meditation, yoga, cardio workouts, or diets that include nutritious food and elimination of sugar and highly processed foods. Despite the method chosen to help become more focused, eventually, being more persistent is up to the individual.

Another key to being persistent is to surround yourself with people who can and will support you in the quest to reach your goals. Negative Nellies need not apply.

Identifying positive, can-do, people may be a challenge for some. The easiest way to find optimists is to ask your candidates some exploratory questions. Here are a few to get you started:

1. Would you describe yourself as a positive person? (Note: This is to determine if they are capable of being supportive. If they are of the negative persuasion, chances are they will see all glasses as half full. Time to keep searching.)

2. What helps you to focus and be persistent?

3. How did you pace yourself when you had a long journey ahead to reach your goal? Could you remain persistent for a sustained period of time? What were your tricks?

4. Do you know anyone who has already achieved the goal(s) I am determined to reach?

5. Would you be willing to help/guide/support me during a certain identified time period?

For some people, like me, it's helpful to create a vision of the goal — one to keep in mind throughout the quest.

I have been writing professionally for years for technology-oriented companies, as well as for numerous other firms in a variety of industries. When I found out one of my articles was going to be published in *Money Magazine,* I recognized it as an acknowledgement by a publication I respected, one that reciprocated their respect for my business knowledge. I did not have a particular topic in mind when I started writing business articles, but instead envisioned reaching an audience that could relate to what I had to share.

Reaching this level of professional acknowledgement has taken me years. I had been persistently pursuing this goal for about a year. Prior to setting the goal to have my writing appear in a professional business publication, my dream was just that. But as the saying goes, a dream without a goal is just a wish.

Thanks to my persistence and optimism, I have earned the recognition that comes after working for years in what could be referred to as the professional trenches. The fact my article debuted on Halloween was a real treat!

## Getting Ahead By Making Mistakes

*Why do some people believe that making mistakes and asking for help is a big no-no? They are two of the best skills you can learn. Every mistake you make serves as a building block toward the next success. Fear of making a mistake can be a barrier to taking any action — and one which prevents any learning from occuring.*

One of a friend's favorite book, *Lessons From the Art of Juggling*, describes how important making mistakes is to creating success. Authors Tony Buzan and Michael J. Gelb write that learning to juggle includes accepting the fact that you're going to drop the ball, and that that's okay. It's necessary. Nobody can juggle on the very first try!

If there is one exasperating thing I have witnessed for years, it is seeing anyone struggling with something for hours, yet not asking for help to accelerate the process and finish the task. They are experiencing the S.H.A.M.E. syndrome — "Should Have Already Mastered Everything." No one knows everything. Find someone who *does* know what you need to accomplish the task and ask for help.

I know some people only learn if they "try" to do it themselves; but let's face it, numerous hours are wasted because people are afraid to ask for assistance. Imagine how much more they could learn if they asked for help instead of struggling through a task they do not yet know how to do?

I am also annoyed by a perception that making mistakes has only a negative connotation. If there is one major tip I can share with you about life and business, it is that the best way to learn and to advance in your career is to make mistakes.

Others believe that if you are not making mistakes, you are not trying hard enough, and are playing it way too safe. In *Lessons from the Art of Juggling*, Buzan, a learning consultant and author of *The Mind Map Book*, and Gelb, an experienced juggler and learning consultant as well, submit that learning to juggle requires failure. If you're not dropping the ball, you're not learning.

Stop playing it safe. Make mistakes. Ask for help. Yes, it's that simple.

Rarely is anyone fired for making a mistake or asking for help. I know when I have admitted to needing help or to making a mistake, I have always benefitted tremendously. At first, it was intimidating to ask for help, and incredibly humbling to admit I had made a mistake; but the net result far outweighed playing it safe. I have also never fired anyone for making mistakes or for asking for help. Actually, I promoted most of the people who did both of these things!

And here's another secret: Your boss or colleagues really do want to help. Studies show that people derive far more satisfaction from helping someone versus not doing so. Think about the last time you helped someone. Didn't you feel better afterwards? Since we all have only 24 hours each day why not make the most of your time and be as productive as possible. Consider the expression, "Fail fast" — simple, yet impactful. When we make mistakes, we typically learn more than we do by sticking to the same old routine.

For myself, unless I am trying new things, making mistakes, and constantly challenging myself, I feel I am wasting my time. But I also assure you that I have had a far richer professional experience as a result.

I am dyslexic. I did not find this out officially until I was 21 years old, but I always knew I learned and thought differently than everyone around me. The good news was that as a result of having a learning disability, I knew I needed to ask for help to keep up, or to better understand what I was supposed to be doing. Becoming comfortable asking for help was an essential survival method in both life and business. I quickly realized I did not have to know everything, and also became aware that I should rely upon others who were far better at doing certain things than I was. Appreciating the fact others had strengths I did not have was something I also learned by asking for help, usually as a result of making a mistake. If someone could not help me, they generally knew who could.

To get ahead in both life and business, start becoming comfortable making mistakes and asking for help. It is far easier to do than you might imagine, and I wish someone had given me as advice early on or at some point in my career.

## How to Build Your Reliability Reputation

*All businesses run on the concept of being reliable, of having trustworthy employees. Being reliable is something that cannot be taken for granted. Learn a few ways to increase your reliability reputation, and how to teach others to be more reliable.*

Not everyone is completely reliable all the time. Some may be close to perfect, while most just do their best. We are all human and although we might strive for perfection, there is no such thing. Earning a reputation for being reliable is a desired trait, and one that takes time to acquire.

One of the pillars of a successful business is reliability. The concept comes in a variety of flavors. Let's focus on human reliability. Without reliability as an embraced (strategy, hypotheses, belief) in an organization, by all members, the fundamentals of running the business simply will not thrive.

On a recent trip to Australia, I witnessed how the concept of reliability plays such a critical role. The 16-hour flight provided many opportunities to think about reliability and to see it in action. The amazing Qantas flight crew worked in harmony and relied upon each other to do their jobs. If you think about all of the elements associated with what it takes to get a large commercial plane off the ground, and the incredible amount of details which need to be executed to make this possible, what a wonderful demonstration of teamwork and reliability.

When people are doing their jobs well — and most are reliant upon others to some degree, amazing things can happen. Conversely, when team members lose sight of the fact that being unreliable can have negative consequences that will impact others, bad things can happen. That's bad news on the ground, but in the air? No!

This may seem incredibly basic from a common-sense perspective, but more often than you think, you or your colleagues lose sight of the power of reliability.

So, how do you stay focused on being reliable? Staying focused is easier if you care about your work performance. What's more, doing a great job is going to help not only you, but others, now, and in the future.

One way to stay focused is to break your tasks into segments — about 30 to 45 minutes is ideal, as most people start to lose their ability to focus well past this point. Not all jobs will allow you to pause and take a short break, but if you are fortunate enough to be able to do this, the result will be of a higher quality, and you will have renewed energy for resuming the assignment. Your colleagues will likely also be impressed with the outcome, and you will begin to build your reputation for producing quality work. More importantly, you will have an enviable reliability rating!

Another way to remain focused is to segment the type of tasks you tackle. For example, consider checking email at the beginning, middle, and end of the day versus constantly checking messages throughout the day.

If you have the type of work that requires you to be in meetings, whenever possible, plan them at the beginning of the day. That leaves the remainder of the afternoon to accomplish the assignments for which you are responsible.

Save the work you enjoy most for the end of the day. This way, you will have it to look forward to, and, because it is the type of work you like, you will have a renewed sense of energy.

Another trick to remaining focused is to take brisk walks around the office. Consider these jaunts as mini rewards for accomplishing the task on which you were working. Plus, any kind of exercise is a bonus, and who knows who you'll meet!

Being considered reliable is a designation you earn from your colleagues. When you demonstrate to others that you are reliable, your entire team or the company you work for will benefit. Think about a time when you had to rely upon someone and they did not follow through. Not desirable, right? And it made you think twice about being able to rely upon that person again. Keep the concept of reliability in mind the next time you are tasked with a responsibility for doing anything related to your job. It helps to keep you focused on a much more positive outcome, and your colleagues will enjoy working with you even more than they already do!

*Dedicated to Elfi at Qantas Airlines. Thanks for your inspiration!*

## Tapping Into Common Sense

*I have often said I wish there was a school for common sense, but unfortunately there is not one yet. Why? Because so many people seem to lack basic common sense. Are you one of them and no one has told you?*

Over the years, I have often wondered why there is not a school for common sense, and why a course on this topic is not offered in middle or high school. For fun, I have periodically searched on-line to find a class on common sense. Typically, this is prompted by an act by someone I know, or based on an interaction shared by someone else about the "lack of common sense" exhibited by another individual or colleague.

There are so many examples of people who do not have common sense or who, from time to time, say or do something which would be classified as nonsensical. The real question is, does someone who lacks common sense know they fall into this classification?

Is common sense a gift or a natural ability some people possess (e.g., an ability to draw, dance, are mechanically inclined, have a good sense of direction) or can it be taught?

If, for the sake of conversation, we agree this subject can be taught, where would you even begin as it is such a broad reaching topic? Perhaps the subject could be broken down into various categories such as at home, at work, in social settings, with friends, family, pets, or while traveling outside of the U.S. borders.

The point is, there needs to be a foundation or entry-level course, and hypothetically, there also needs to be an instructor who is deemed to have an enormous amount of good judgment to teach the course.

Common sense involves finding solutions to scenarios, and the brain's ability to think through a series of steps to come up with an ideal resolution. However, every brain is wired and processes information differently, so the potential to have multiple solutions to a problem is entirely possible.

Unfortunately, not all solutions are equal. This is often when the process devised and presented has what I will refer to as "gaps" that may not be ideally suited to solve the challenge. An example of this could be that your boss decides to routinely schedule non-essential meetings when most people are in the process of wrapping up their day. The meetings could easily be held during regular business hours, or the information could be presented in a written format instead of a face-to-face meeting, especially if the meetings are not about time-sensitive topics. Instead, she decides to call you at 11 p.m. on Friday to ask you to begin working on the notes from the meeting. A person with common sense would know they can and should wait until Monday morning to obtain this information from you.

Another example of having common sense would include knowing when to stay home from work when you are sick. We have sick days for a reason, and they also protect your colleagues from getting sick, missing work, and secretly being mad at you for coming to work and exposing them to your illness. No one wants to be sick, so if you are visibly and noticeably sick, common sense would inform you to stay home.

So, if there was a test to determine whether you had common sense, would you want to take it? Or, have there been times you wish you could send someone you know or whom you have encountered to "Common Sense School?" I guarantee most people who possess common sense would answer *yes* to this question.

# Who's Real and Who's Faking It?

*Can you spot someone who is "faking it" at the office? How can you tell if someone is really who they say they are, has the knowledge they profess to have, and who is, in fact, the "real deal."*

Have you ever been in a meeting with a colleague and thought, "Does this person *really* know what they are doing or talking about?" Was it your boss?

When I first started out in business, I would have rarely questioned someone's authority or professional knowledge. I also presumed those who held a higher-ranking position than mine knew what they were talking about and doing, and had earned their way into this role. News flash! I was wrong, and boy, was I naïve. I thought everyone earned their way into their position and had the battle scars to prove it.

Unfortunately, my early career reasoning about authenticity was far from the truth. I soon realized, through experience, that there are many people in the business world and other industries who are faking it every day.

Over the years, I have honed my fake-o-meter skills to properly detect who is the real deal and who is just blustering along. How did I learn to do this? By asking multiple questions and not accepting all information shared by the presumed authority as being the truth or even credible. Posing multi-faceted questions about the information being shared, you will either intrigue them with your curiosity, or annoy them with unexpected challenges.

If the person seems annoyed, there is a strong chance they are misrepresenting the information. They may also get defensive, try to change the subject, or tell you they have to do something else immediately to avoid being caught on your fake-o-meter radar.

There are a number of other ways to detect if a person is authentic. Recently, a friend told me about a Netflix show called "Lie to Me." The show is about a guy and his colleagues who have mastered the art and even created a profession of detecting if someone is telling the truth.

Several ways they do this include reading facial expressions and body language. They start by watching the subject's eyes – looking down or away often indicates they are misrepresenting the truth. Excessive swallowing, clenching hands, rapid speech, fidgeting, and sweating or having a difficult time making a point are also signs your meter should be sending loud signals.

Relying upon your intuition, your gut, and your emotional intelligence skills should not be overlooked as additional strategies to spot imposters.

Another simple question you can ask is, "Why did you say that?" Or, ask for proof about the source of their information. If you detect they are continuing to spin a web of deceit during your conversation, they probably are.

Naturally, there are people who I would classify as professional purveyors of crap ("BS" artists); we have all encountered them. There are also people who have sociopathic tendencies and cannot help themselves from embellishing the truth or creating a story not based on reality. Realistically, this is a small portion of our population. If you come across one, you will likely be fooled, as they have mastered the art of deception. Take comfort in the fact that you're not alone. Sometimes they do get caught.

More often, people who are faking it are doing so to preserve their professional reputation or to avoid embarrassment for not knowing what they should know.

Over the course of time, you will inevitably come across a person or multiple people who are faking it. The next time it happens, celebrate, as you now have some methods to establish whether the person is credible, or if you have come across a fast-talking, smooth-as-silk, con artist.

Good luck turning on your personal fake-o-meter, and don't be afraid to put it to the test.

# Are You Really Listening?

*Most people would admit they are not good listeners. If they were, they would be amazed at what they hear when they really listen. Listening well and reading body language go hand in hand to provide you with opportunities. Are you capitalizing on these skills?*

How many times have you caught yourself drifting off during a conversation, not really listening with your full attention or crafting a response as the other person spoke! Have you ever considered how much information you might be missing when you are only semi listening? When you are actively listening and fully engaged in the conversation, you will be amazed at how much satisfaction and insight you can gain.

A friend relayed a heartwarming story about a conversation he had with one of his patients a few years ago. The woman was receiving physical therapy to relieve chronic pain. She was in the final stage of her life. Despite the agony, she was the type of person who was always thinking of others, especially her family.

During one of her sessions with my friend, let's call him Dave, the woman revealed a wish she had for her son. Her son, let's call him Joe, had been a hockey player all his life. When he went through a divorce, Joe's ex-wife got rid of all of his hockey gear. He was a goalie, so the equipment was expensive. Playing hockey brought joy to Joe's life, but with no equipment, and no money to replace it, he stopped playing and became disheartened.

The woman passed away, but Dave remembered her story, because he was actively engaged and listening to her. Within a year of her death, Dave, who is also a hockey player, remembered his client's dying wish of having her son getting back into playing hockey. He devised a way to fulfill that wish. He purchased some used goalie equipment and put it into a gym bag, then found out where Joe lived. One day, he showed up on Joe's doorstep with a bag full of goalie gear. Joe could not believe a total stranger had done this for him, and was overwhelmed with emotion.

Once total strangers, Dave and Joe became best buds. This friendship developed out of Dave's ability to truly listen, and to go a step further and do something with the information. Since the day Joe received this generous gift, he has been playing and enjoying hockey once again.

What if there were more people like Dave, who really listened and followed through on what they heard? We all have the capacity to do this, and do it well. In the business world, it is imperative to our success that we become skilled listeners. Although it may seem like an easy thing to do, listening and doing it well takes practice and dedication.

One of my favorite sayings is from Epictetus: "I was given two ears, and one mouth. That means I should listen twice as much as I speak."

We live in a world of constant distraction and endless interruptions, so having focused conversations can be a challenge; however, paying attention is imperative, and when you do, the end results can be as rewarding as the story about my friend Dave and Joe.

One trick I use when actively listening is to take notes. It is not always possible, but when I have, being able to refer back to my scribbles, bullet points, and arrows from the conversation is remarkable. It allows me to think through what was being said from a different dimension, and most times to come up with a better outcome as a result.

Most business conversations, in general, are a way to convey information, and often are a way to figure out a solution to either a problem or an issue one or both participants are experiencing. All of us have the ability to solve challenges, and we can do so more quickly and efficiently when we are actively engaged.

So, the next time you are in a conversation or a meeting, take a moment to consider whether you are fully listening. If you are not, refocus your attention and know that when you do this, each party will significantly benefit.

*This story is dedicated to Doug Kennedy.*

## More Kindness, Please

*We are bombarded with sad and tragic news every day. Not surprisingly, this carries over into our moods and what we are thinking about while we are working. What if you could do your part to help offset this reality? Something that would make everyone with whom you interact experience a random act of kindness?*

With all the sad news overwhelming us seemingly every day, I wondered what I could do to help to offset all the negative vibes in our world. Me. Just little me.

We can all certainly use an infusion of kindness and positivity in our lives. What can we do to begin a chain reaction of inciting more acts of kindness? The trick will be to not become complacent and stop being kind to others each day. Here is my list of acts of kindness. Please feel free to borrow and implement generously:

1. Smile at everyone you see and say hello to them, too. Yes, *everyone*.

2. Bring in some treats, healthy ones if you can, to share with your colleagues. You may inspire others to participate.

3. Buy a bouquet of flowers and put a single blossom in a small cup of water. Place one on as many people's desks as possible. I actually did this one day, and passed out over 40 flowers, without telling anyone. The reaction people had about receiving a single bloom was amazing. It was so much fun to see how happy this simple act made them.

4. Bring in an item or items from your home to be donated. Put them in a box, ask others to contribute as well, and then take the full box to your favorite charity.

5. Send your colleagues an e-card. There are a number of free options online. Check them out!

6. If you have a special talent, offer to share your skills or teach co-workers during a break, or prior to or after work.

7. Take some photos of your colleagues at work, share them, and then let each person decide what to do next. If they have kids, it might be

fun for them to see an action photo of them at work.

8. Have some extra books around your house? Bring them in to share with your colleagues. Leave them in a public place with a note that they are for others to enjoy. They can keep them, pass them along, or bring them back in for others to read.

9. If you have access to tickets of any kind, offer to give them to the first person who sends you an email to claim them. The tickets could even be to a middle or high school play or concert.

10. Offer to donate an hour of your time to a colleague outside of work who might need help with a project. Maybe they are moving, or need help assembling new furniture or fixing their car.

11. Celebrate co-workers' birthdays and accomplishments — even the ones that might seem insignificant. The point is to have more celebrations just for the sake of creating smiles and opportunities for people to focus on something positive. And bring that camera!

12. Genuinely compliment as many people as possible during the course of a day. It could be something as simple as they have neat handwriting, or are always on time to meetings.

This list is clearly only a start, but one I hope will be a catalyst for others.

It's true — we can change the world one random act of kindness at a time. What will you do to brighten someone's day?

## How to Stay Passionate About Your Career

*Finding your passion and then pursuing a career aligned with it has been in vogue for the last decade. Colleges, career counselors, and HR professionals routinely give out the advice to "follow your passion." It makes sense to align your passion with your career or employment aspirations, but it may not be as easy as it sounds. Or is it?*

When I think back to finding my passion, I realize it began when I studied Advertising in college in the School of Journalism. Because I was always interested in print, radio, and television advertising, it made perfect sense for me to learn more about this subject. I recall always being fascinated by how each product, service or brand told its story, or value proposition via words, images and sounds.

I enjoyed the narrative of each advertisement, and the sheer delight in assigning my own grade to each advertisement I encountered. This was fun! When I was faced with declaring my major, I will never forget how fellow University of Maine student, Gary Huffnagle, said he chose Advertising as his major because it combined both writing and a creative element that could be expressed visually, verbally, or via a combination. His enthusiasm for the major, the type of classes he was taking, and the fact I was always interested in advertising, made it the obvious choice for me to follow in his footsteps.

But my degree in Journalism was also a practical degree. I also knew I could find a job with the skills it provided. This degree allowed me to practice and master my communication abilities in the business world, and opened the proverbial door for me into having a marketing career.

Most of the expertise I acquired was via hands-on learning experiences. For example, I will never forget in one of my early jobs the company was going to a trade show. It was up to me to figure out how to get us there, and everything this entailed. I also vividly recall learning about social and digital media marketing as at that time it was becoming a new way to reach an audience; writing my first press release; and holding my first press conference without any guidance on how to do either.

My point is that because of my passion, I was fearless when it came to trying new things. Each new experience gave me more confidence to try another task with which I had little to no expertise. Best of all, it never felt like work — and this may be one of the key elements to knowing if you have found your passion. You know the phrase: "If you do something you love, you'll never work a day in your life."

Sure, there are other things in my life I adore — real estate, interior design, coaching/mentoring people; but when I truly think about what I am rock solid passionate about, it is Marketing. The fact this field is so varied and offers such a diverse amount of options to pursue advertising, channel, communications, content, demand generation, digital, events, graphic design, international, operations, product marketing, public relations, web site design, is what has held my attention for the length of time it has.

Marketing has been a perfect profession for me because it has also allowed me to work with so many different business disciplines — Accounting, Customer Service, Engineering, HR, Product Marketing/Management, and Sales — and to learn more about how the various departments function together. It's diverse, it's fascinating, and I'm constantly eager to learn more.

Whether you're just starting out, or making a decision to change careers, think about the subjects that make your heart beat faster, such as travel, music, design, running, baking, etc. Now think about the fields associated with these subjects. Then make a list of all of the types of jobs that are aligned, even slightly, with the subject. Once you have your list, narrow it down to your top three.

Finally, begin asking people you know to introduce you to folks who have jobs associated with your top areas of interest. Ask them about how they got started, and what first-steps advice they could offer.

Most importantly, have fun with this! I guarantee you will find motivation on your journey to learn more about the topics you listed. You can then, ideally, begin your path towards pursuing your passion via a career which will hold your interest for many years to come.

*Thanks to Tom Snelders for encouraging me to write, and by picking this topic from my list of topics to write about.*

## Is Work/Life Balance a Myth?

*It seems like it should be easy to achieve a work/life balance. Everyone talks about wanting to have this balance, but is it realistic to think it's possible, or does the concept belong in the urban myth category?*

Work–life balance incorporates proper prioritization between work (career and ambition) and lifestyle (health, pleasure, leisure, family). It refers to an ability to maintain a healthy balance between work, personal responsibilities, and family life in a time when we can access work emails and assignments 24/7.

Not everyone who writes about balancing your life actually has street cred, but I do. My credentials include raising various offspring — one college grad, one college co-ed, and one high schooler; plus my furry baby, AKA our five-year-old Golden Doodle, as well as a frog and lizard. I also have a husband whose office is 200 miles from our house and who has commuted there for four years; and also a sister, a brother, a Mom and Dad and in-laws, as well as relatives from their relationships.

I am fortunate to have friends I met as far back in elementary school in the fourth grade (Greg, Kathy and Monique), relationships I have maintained while working full-time in the demanding high-tech marketing industry.

Balancing all of this has not been easy, but I would not trade my experiences for anything. Being a full-time working mother puts one in a position of constantly weighing the pros and cons of decisions on an hourly basis, sometimes simultaneously both at work and home. So, it has been critical for me to be able to have my family reach me at all times, meaning my mobile phone is always turned on and always close by. There have also been numerous times during my career when I have excused myself during important professional conversations when my children or other family members have reached out.

Yes, this might seem impolite, but I prioritize my family over work 100% of the time. No job or career is worth the reverse, especially if you are in a field that demands you work excessively long hours.

Friends are another part of the equation, which you should never forget to maintain as part of your work/life balance. I have seen too many people compromise relationships because they are unable to simply send a text once in awhile to their friends to let them know they are thinking about them.

Proper amounts of sleep, nutrition, and exercise are also fundamental aspects of obtaining work/life balance. Yes, there are times when each of these will be compromised; but the point is to maintain as much discipline as you can making these aspects of your life a priority, too. At times when I was averaging five to six hours of sleep at night, not able to exercise, or eat properly, I paid dearly by feeling overly stressed, exhausted, and at the mercy of my schedule or life.

With help from friends and family, and by reprioritizing these aspects of my life, I was able to get back on track and have my life come back into balance. Again, this was not easy. Be kind to yourself and don't become overly frustrated when you get out of balance.

You also have to realize you are not a super hero. It is fine to ask for help from others, as you can reciprocate when they will need you at some point. Always remember that you are a human being, not a human doing.

Of course, there are other facets of life to factor into the mix; but this is the fun part. The trick is to schedule them: write them down, create a To Do list, etc. I have found that if I write something down, it will get done.

Once it is on paper, or on a calendar, or in the phone, it is like a personal "up-front-contract" to adhere to and to make happen. Perhaps not in the exact time frame I wanted it to, but as close to when it would be possible to accomplish the item (e.g., travel, coach and see our kids participate in their sporting or other activities, take a course, work on my hobbies, go to the gym, spend quality time with family/friends, etc.).

I am not saying my life is perfect, as I do not think there is such a thing, but I do believe you can strike a balance in your life and accomplish more than you imagine is possible.

*Thanks to Holden Laquerre and Patrick Sweeney for encouraging me to write, and by picking this topic from my list of topics to write about next.*

## Success:  What's Your Definition?

*Success can be defined in many ways.  Don't limit yourself to only one or two of them.  Create your own definition of success and see what happens, and how much better your life can be.*

Graduation.  It happens every year.  Whether it's from high school or college, or perhaps from another program that concludes with a diploma, the inevitable question is, "What's next?"

Why can't people skip this question and accept the act of graduating is, in fact, an act of success?  Many might, but graduation should be further recognized and celebrated for longer than simply the commencement ceremony.

Fast forward past graduation and into the "working world."  Here's where many young graduates and parents begin to stress out about how they or their grads are defining themselves from a success perspective.

Here are some questions that might be swirling through their brains:

- *Have I accepted a position at the right company?*
- *Am I on the "fast track" to move up the career ladder?*
- *Am I networking with enough people?*
- *Am I networking with the right people?*
- *How do I feel, physically and mentally?*
- *How genuine are my friendships?  Will they last?*
- *Do I have a family or network to support me in times of celebration or crisis?*
- *Do I enhance another person's life because of my presence or support?*

This may not be the best use of energy, because if you study truly successful people, they often say it really doesn't fully matter what you are doing early in your career.  The point is to do the best you can do in the role you are in, and to leverage this role as a stepping stone, unless you are in a field which requires a strictly defined path like nursing, engineering, teaching, and more.

Success can be defined many ways. I challenge you not to be boxed-in and limited by others, or via the more traditional methods of how success in numerous first world countries — money, fame, status — is defined.

Instead, try a new perspective and think about success in smaller, more bite-sized pieces, or in terms of achieving success by other methods, such as physical and mental health, the depth and breadth of your friendships, your family or other support network, or your ability to improve or enhance another person's life simply by your presence and support.

Yes, success is often thought of in monetary terms of status and achievement, but what if money and status did not matter? Could you then define success as achieving happiness each day, or perhaps everyone on the planet being kind and accepting of each other?

Perhaps success could be defined simply by ticking off all the boxes on your daily "to do list" or teaching another person about something they did not know. Stop stressing out about how success is defined by others, or by standards you have had ingrained into you since childhood.

Take time to create your own definition of success. Do not empower others to do this on your behalf. You will only end up being disappointed, as someone else's definition of success is always going to be different from your own. Stop comparing yourself to others.

## Life at the Top: Is the View Worth the Effort?

*Going after what you want professionally can be exhilarating and rewarding. But it also has a down side, as the journey of getting to the top will inevitably put you in a position others envy, and who you likely surpassed to get there. Is it worth climbing to the top of whatever ladder you decide to climb?*

Climbing the proverbial career ladder is not for everyone. But if you have even a one competitive bone in your body, the thought has certainly crossed your mind. Plotting and planning how to escalate the ladder is not always a straight-forward process. In many business disciplines, there are few clear paths or methods that guarantee how to get to the top.

I am not a fan of politics, but realize there is a fair amount of politics with which one has to contend in order to scale the rungs. Essentially, politics is a popularity contest. You need to figure out how to deal with the people who are in influential roles. It's likely they will have a say in whether you will be able to ascend or not.

Having political "supporters" is critical to successfully navigate in a corporation heavily laden with politics. Unfortunately, a company does not need to be large to have politics influence its culture, and how its employees rise or become stagnant.

When I ask CEOs and other top-level executives if their journey was worth it, a large percentage tell me no. More than half said they had to sacrifice so much personally to get where they are. Although there are certainly advantages at the top, as we all know, money cannot buy happiness. Some executives told me they would trade their position or do things differently if they could get back to a simpler life and feel happy again.

And while we are on the subject…happiness is not something you can simply just want to have. You have to work at being happy. The first step is to determine what makes you happy. Prepare a mental list, and you just might realize that you already have everything you need to be happy. Indeed, when I talk to CEOs about what makes them happy, they often realize there are a few things they could alter to get back to feeling happy again.

Climbing the professional ladder can take years. Most people will need new skills. Many will likely switch departments or employers two or more times. Why? Because typically, when someone moves into a different role, they will acquire new skills and valuable experiences not always available when they remain at a specific position or company for more than a few years. They will also see things differently in a new environment, be exposed to new people, and learn new approaches to their work.

Change is not something with which everyone feels comfortable, but those who embrace and become comfortable with change are typically the ones who climb the career ladder over their peers who do not. Slow and steady is a great concept for the majority of people in an organization, and thankfully, many people are satisfied with this operating style. If everyone wanted to rise to the top there would be serious management issues to address. Luckily, this typically is not the case. There are layers of management built into the organization at larger companies, in part to control or even prevent this from happening.

The next time you think about whether you are ready to climb the corporate ladder, decide how high you'd like to go. Then plot out how you will get there. You can do this by talking to others who are in roles above you not just at your own company, but also at other firms, as there are usually more ways than one to get to where you want to be.

Talking to people can mean actually having a conversation with them in person, or via email or Skype, if distance is a challenge. Ask if they had help planning how they got to where they are, or if the process happened in an organic way. That is often the case if a company routinely promotes employees based on having a well-defined process.

Unfortunately, most companies do not have a systematic, fair, and non-political promotion plan. If your company does not, take comfort knowing that you are in the majority of people who have to figure out how to climb to the top, if this is really what you want to do, and if the top, or even the next rung, is worth the effort.

# Chapter 3 | Life

## Are You Curious Enough?

*Do you ever wonder if you are curious enough about the world around you? Does it matter how curious you are?*

Last week, a friend of mine told me about a young man who passed away on March 28, 2017. He had been battling addiction for many years. When I attended his wake, his entire family told me they were happy he was finally at peace. Anyone who has ever suffered from an illness, or been witness to someone else who has, understands the concept of peace better than most.

Thinking more about this concept led me to explore the topic of curiosity, as I wanted to better understand the true meaning of peace. There are a number of interpretations of the word peace. As a noun, the definition states it means "freedom from disturbance; quiet and tranquility."

I believe this is the meaning the young man's family embraced to express their feelings about an extraordinarily sad occasion. I also imagine this word and concept helped them to come to terms with the situation.

On a lighter note, thank goodness for the Internet and the ease of being able to research information, especially since I have always been curious about many topics. Pre-internet, the challenge to do research took far more effort, and the results did not always satisfy my quest to go layers deep into exploring a topic.

Given the fact I am, by nature, a curious person, I have often wondered if most people are as well? To set the stage on the meaning of the word *curiosity*, according to Wikipedia's definition, "Curiosity is a quality related to inquisitive thinking such as exploration, investigation, and learning, evident by observation in humans and other animals."

Others would likely agree there are varying degrees of curiosity, and times in our lives when we have the opportunity to be more curious. The American proverb "curiosity killed the cat" is a negative connotation of curiosity. If you've already read my artice on positivity, you know where I stand.

Of course, upon researching if there was a follow-up to this statement, I found out via Wikipedia that, "A less frequently-seen rejoiner to 'Curiosity killed the cat' is 'but satisfaction brought it back.'" This must be why I pursue my curiosity quest on a daily basis: Finding out more information about a topic is highly satisfying.

Regardless of who you are, being a curious person has amazing advantages, particularly from a learning perspective, and I love to learn new things. It is my *raison d'etre*.

The challenge of researching topics of interest is always a fascinating process. I am thoroughly amazed each time about what I learn. Is it possible to be too curious? I do not think it is, and my belief is when I stop being curious, my life will not be as rich. There are numerous other advantages to being curious, as is it does not matter what gender you are, your age, your educational background, where you live, or what access you have to information.

As a business person, doing research is an integral and on-going process, as it is critical to learn as much about the industry I am in, the target markets I pursue, the competition and global or closer-to-home events that might have an impact on my business, or the products and services I market.

Thankfully, doing research fueled by my curiosity makes it a pleasurable aspect to my daily activities. And, I cannot imagine if I did not have the drive to be curious every day. Are you curious enough, or does it matter whether or not you are?

*This story is in memory of Torin Michael Lekan of Chelmsford, Massachusetts who passed away at the age of 32. To honor his memory, his family asked people to please help a friend in need.*

# The Impact of Positive Thinking

*Does positive thinking make a difference in your life?*
*I firmly believe it does.*

The power of positive thinking has been written about for years, by many well-known experts on this topic including Mahatma Gandhi, Dr. Norman Vincent Peale, author of *The Power of Positive Thinking*, and the Dalai Lama. I was first exposed to the impact of positivity from my mother, Emily R. Murphy.

Mom had a long career in nursing, including almost a decade in Oncology. As I was growing up, she would tell me stories about the power of positive thinking, especially as it related to healing and her patients. She told me she was gifted in her ability to help people deal with their cancer, and for many years I did not fully understand or appreciate what this meant.

As you would imagine, most of her cancer patients were extremely sick, and some were at the early stages of dealing with this awful disease. According to my mother, the difference between patients and how they handled this dreadful disease was attitude.

The second thing that differentiated her patients from one another was how much they were able to apply positive thinking on a daily basis in even the smallest of ways. Successful were those who were, for example, able to see and appreciate beautiful trees outside of their hospital window, emblazoned with the fall colors for which New England is known.

Ironically, when I looked for lists of well-known optimists, there was not a definitive compilation. But we all know they exist, and I happen to be one of them (although I am not yet known globally for this ability). You see, according to Tom Rath's *Strengths Finder 2.0*, my number one character trait is "Positivity." And I firmly believe your quality of life rests on whether or not you possess an optimistic or positive outlook on life.

There have been numerous instances when, if I thought about the possible outcome of a situation, more than 95 percent of the time the situation turned out to be positive. Is this because I viewed the outcome as being positive, or was it in reality this way? Am I simply a lucky person? Or, did my positive thinking influence the outcome, and my optimistic nature have me only see the outcome as being positive, or the "glass half full?"

My perspective and reality has been that the situations I wanted to have positive outcomes generally turned out that way. If the final result was not positive, there was usually a reason why — timing, location, or another factor over which I had little control.

But even in these instances, my viewpoint greatly impacted my perception of the situation, which ultimately seemed less negative than I thought it would be. I accept the fact that while I don't always get what I want, I do get just what I need.

Based on what Mom witnessed as a nurse time and time again — what some might call miracles — she would state that the power of positive thinking or being optimistic in even the most dire situations can bring you results you did not think possible.

Today's challenge? Pick a day to think about having everything turn out well, and see what that feels like. If you are not a positive person by nature, you might need to start more slowly and take this challenge on by the hour.

Being positive may take practice, but the long-term benefits and the outcomes are totally worth the effort. Take my word, as those who truly know me will tell you, I am living proof of this concept working!

*Thanks to Greg DeGuglielmo and Holden Laquerre for inspiring me to write, and by choosing this topic for me.*

## Random Acts of Kindness

*What was the last random act of kindness you bestowed? Wouldn't the world be a much better place if everyone, each day, did one nice thing for another human? This story is dedicated to the concept of kicking off or planting the seed to dedicate one day a year, or one week each month to doing "random-act-of-kindness" and making it part of our daily routine. Are you on board?*

Do you ever think about the concept of Karma and whether it's real? The Hindu and Buddhism religions do. In the simplest terms, believers define it as a bank account of positive credits for good deeds, and withdrawals associated with less-than-desirable actions. According to this concept, a human's fate will be based on the balance of their Karma Bank at the end of their current life.

There's merit to this concept from a fundamental perspective of trying to do the right thing, and not cause harm to others.

In the business world, a company may be judged and perceived as being society friendly with a positive Karma balance if they are giving back to the community. They earn Karma credit by making monetary donations, or allowing employees to volunteer their time on company hours. Both the company and the employees who are involved with positive community interactions benefit. The higher the level the engagement, the greater the positive feeling the employees have about their company as being a great one to work for.

Yes, it can be expensive for a firm to allow its employees to volunteer time while they are on-the-clock. Not all companies are able to do this; but there are other ways to give back to a community. A few examples would be to organize a drive to collect items for a food bank, or clothing and toiletry donations for a homeless shelter. Collecting pet supplies for an area animal shelter is another option.

Who is keeping track of the Karma points being earned? Does it really matter whether anyone is? You know yourself if there are days or weeks when you or others around you are earning or having points taken out of their Karma bank. On days when you are making more deposits than withdrawals, I bet you feel much better and more fulfilled personally.

Doing nice things for other people, especially when they least expect it, is what I wish more people would consider doing. Random acts of kindness. Wouldn't it be wonderful if every day each of us committed to doing something kind or nice "just because?"

Recently, I had an opportunity to do something unexpected for a group of strangers walking through a park. I overheard them saying they wished they could be flying a kite like I was. Being the extrovert I am, I asked them if they would really like to fly a kite? I had an extra one in my car. In full disclosure, each kite only cost one dollar, but does it really matter how much it cost?

The point is that these three people were amazed by the fact I gave them a kite they could queue up in five minutes and be flying it at the park like I was. The expression of amazement on their faces that I had and was going to give them a kite was such an uplifting feeling. I couldn't stop smiling when I saw how joyful they were (and how much better they were at it than I was). Seeing their kite soaring higher than mine made me really happy.

Funny thing is, I think they might have actually been happier, as it was a complete surprise to them they would be doing this on a Sunday afternoon.

The element of surprise and delight are two fairly easy things to bestow upon other people. How wonderful would it be to see more Karma-related examples in professional environments where this concept is often an underserved or underutilized one.

My hope is that more people do their part in trying to add Karma points to their bank each day.

## The Gift of Time

*When was the last time you thought about the concept of time, and how much of it you really have? Are you using your time wisely and treating it as a precious gift?*

There is a time in our life when we feel we have infinitely more time than we might, particularly when we are younger than 18. I chose this age because in the U.S. that is when you are legally recognized as an adult.

We all know that no one really knows how much time each of us has to be on this planet. So, what would you do differently if you knew how much time you had left? Would you make a "bucket list" of the things you want to do, or would you not act any differently?

What if you could do exactly what you wanted to do with your time without any consequences? Or, what if you could do only the things which truly made you happy? I began thinking about time and how each of us looks at it from a different perspective, and how it is governed by each of our own life circumstances. Sometimes the choices we make have an impact either positively or negatively on our life, and other times situations occur that are out of our control, suddenly bringing our time to an end.

Recently I attended a funeral of a friend's mother; I listened, captivated, as my friend described her mother's life. I was thoroughly absorbed by her storytelling ability, but what struck me the most was her mother's absolute joyful perspective on the life she had lived.

Not all of her days were a "perfect 10," but this woman clearly knew how to live! As her daughter relayed it, essentially everyone she met, her mother adopted into her life. She did this with the sole purpose of making them feel like they were a gift and special to her. Each day this woman made it her mission to make everyone she engaged with have a better day.

I wish I could tell you I knew my friend's mother well. I did not have that good fortune. I met her in last few minutes of her life as she lay in hospice, surrounded by her family, who had gathered for dinner. She was peacefully resting in her bed behind the kitchen table, joining them in her own way. This family was clearly making the best use of the time they had with her, and showered her with their presence and love.

When you think about time and how you use it, do you think in terms of it being a gift? Today I was reminded that I should think of time that way, and not assume I have an infinite amount of it. Instead, I need to focus on making sure I am capitalizing on each day to the fullest.

Bill Keane has a very fitting statement relating to time. "Yesterday is history, tomorrow is a mystery, today is a gift. That's why we call it the present."

Everyone has a different definition of success; they approach the concept of time similarly. As we get older, the saying "Time flies" takes on a new meaning.

When I was younger, there were days when time felt like it stood still — Christmas Eve, for instance. I am not exactly sure when I realized time was moving at a faster rate, but it was likely when I was in my mid- to late-20s, when I felt the pressure to make various life choices. Looking back on my decisions and their timing, I am glad I chose the way I did. The selections I made are the building blocks that have made me into the person I am today.

I am sad that my friend's mother's passing was a catalyst to make me seriously think about time as a gift, I'm grateful to have gained a new perspective about time.

## Harnessing Anticipation as Motivation

*To motivate you, leverage the energy produced when you are anticipating an outcome.*

As I was trying to motivate myself to continue to work on a project, I thought it would be an interesting twist to see if I could tap into and harness the energy I had from anticipating news I would hear about the following week.

Instead of potentially being anxious about hearing the news and procrastinating my task at hand, I instead considered how I could constructively utilize my anticipation of the news to motivate me in a productive and positive manner. So far so good, as I am sharing this experience with you now, and I hope you can apply my strategy to help harness your anticipation as motivation.

Another way to look at harnessing anticipation was to direct my frustration in waiting for a response, and to again, redirect my energy in a constructive mode. I will admit, I had to think about how to do this, as it was not my first instinct, but the outcome and redirection of my energy is far more rewarding.

One of my articles, "Persistence is a Super Power," also inspired me to write about motivation. I noticed the kind of people and organizations who were reading the original blog — including readers from The Gartner Group and The Boston Red Sox — and was thrilled that well-known companies and brands were benefitting from my blog.

The topics I write about have come from my interest in exploring and learning more about the subject, and to share what I learn with others who might be curious about the subject, too. And sometimes I also ask a select few mentors and friends to choose the next blog topic. Often, it is difficult to decide which one to focus on, as they are all intriguing topics from my perspective, so it comes down to deciding which one I can relate to the most at that moment in time.

Have you ever thought about why you might be more motivated some days, or specific times of the day more than others? I have, and often I attribute my motivation levels to influences such as the weather, whether I am well rested or tired, or if it is the morning, which tends to be the time of day I have the highest level of motivation. I am, indeed, a "morning person."

Regardless of these influences, however, another factor I had not considered was my level of "hope." If I am anticipating hearing about, doing, or going someplace, the concept of how hopeful I am about doing so also plays a significant role in how motivated I am. Have you ever noticed this about yourself?

You may have heard the phrase, "hope is not a strategy." I disagree! Indeed, in the absence of having hope, I become more stressed and less optimistic about the anticipated outcome of a situation. When I am hopeful about something, my attitude and motivation factors are much higher, and I have a sense of the possibility of anticipating an outcome that I can both visualize and desire.

The next time you are faced with a situation when you are anticipating news of any kind, see if you are able to harness the energy derived from the anticipation to motivate you to do something positive or constructive.

## Start Trusting Your Instincts

*It is critical to trust your instincts in business and in life. What steps are you taking to feel confident enough to trust your gut 100 percent of the time?*

One thing Oprah knows for sure is that learning to trust your instincts, using that intuitive sense of what's best for you, is paramount for any lasting success. She believes instinct is "a whispery sensation that pulsates just beneath the surface of your being. All animals have it. We're the only creatures that deny and ignore it."

In his book, *Thinking, Fast and Slow,* author Daniel Kahneman, a Nobel Memorial Prize in Economics laureate, described how our brain works from an instinct perspective. He referenced to how, when we are driving on the highway, we can detect if someone in the car next to us might be dangerous, and how we will instinctively maneuver away from them. This same concept can apply in many scenarios. It actually happens to each of us every day. We all have a natural ability to apply our instincts to help keep ourselves safe and to make decisions based on this internal compass.

How have you used your instincts to determine whether someone is authentically representing themselves? How you can activate your internal fake-o-meter to judge if they are "real?"

People who come across as overly confident are simply braggarts. Sometimes they are so smooth in their delivery, you may be mesmerized and accept their information and them as legitimate. How can you supercharge your ability to tap into your instincts? It takes becoming comfortable with your powerful tool of instinct.

Since there are limited, if any, courses to help people develop fake-o-meter abilities, particularly in the business world, the next best way to hone your innate (or untapped, dormant, hidden) talents is to practice relying upon them.

I guarantee you will be intimidated by relying on your instincts 100 percent, but test driving them in different instances is really the only way to become proficient at leveraging this powerful tool.

I remember the first time someone called me out for not trusting my gut. I was surprised by how they knew I did not trust my instincts. In this particular case, I did not trust my gut about hiring a person. I hired him, despite my misgivings.

Fast forward two to four weeks from the first day. I could clearly see I made my first hiring mistake.

There were others in the office who really wanted this man to join the team, but I had many reservations, mainly driven by instincts I chose to ignore. Big mistake, as the person turned out to be a thief, and worse yet, he had a well-hidden police record buried deep in a Google search. He caused mayhem within the organization for several months until he was actually arrested. (Can you say *drama*?) It was more than I had bargained for, and it is clear now I should have listened to my instincts and not have trusted those of my co-workers.

In an article for the *Harvard Business Review* by former editorial director and executive editor Justin Fox, "Instinct Can Beat Analytical Thinking," he digs deep into what are referred to as heuristics, and really geeks-out about this particular theory based concept on instincts.

I'll spare you the gory details. Essentially, heuristics is about rules of thumb, or gut instincts, that do not rely upon math or statistics to come to a conclusion. The theory suggests other decision-making shortcuts that leverage a person's experience can lead to making better decisions than relying upon scientific modeling.

Today's challenge? Start making decisions based on your gut instincts. Before you take off the proverbial training wheels and rely solely on your intuition, I recommend you sprinkle in a dose of advice from a trusted colleague with a solid history of making sound decisions.

Let me know how well your instincts are working for you, as I always enjoy hearing from my readers.

# Chapter 4 | Tips & Resources

## Finding and Leveraging Your Niche

*No two grains of sands are identical. The same concept can be applied to people. Although many people might have a great deal in common with one another, when you begin to take a closer look, you will quickly see how their differences help define their niche, or who they are.*

Having a niche can serve you well in most competitive scenarios — a lesson I learned while snorkeling in Australia's Great Barrier Reef off of Cairns. My story is a perfect example of how one can apply their niche, and make it work for them. You can apply these same concepts to define your personal or business niche.

My recent snorkling trip was something I have wanted to do for many years. When I was researching which tours to take on my trip of a lifetime, I thought the best way to narrow my search would be to choose based on word of mouth. Since I enjoy posing questions, I started asking people I encountered on the streets of Australia if they had recently been on a reef tour, and, if they had, whether they would recommend it to others. Most people I spoke with had toured with large 100-foot boats that accommodate several hundred people, which was particularly appealing, but too commercial for my liking. Finally, I met someone who had been on a reef tour the day before. When she started describing the experience she had and used the word *quirky* more than a few times, I thought this was definitely something I wanted to experience, too, and I did the next day.

The experience started early in the morning. I arrived at the dock and saw an old-fashioned sailing vessel that looked nothing like any of the other reef tour boats — large, swift catamaran hulls. The captain and crew were also not who you would imagine to be typical crew mates, but they were each beyond amazing at what they did. Two were scuba instructors, two others knew how to sail the boat, and everyone knew how to manage the sails and rigging.

Each also had an amazing personality. Only two were from Australia; the captain was from Miami, one crew member from France, one from Tasmania, and the other had lived in a variety of places, most recently Fiji. Since the boat was only about 55 feet long, the number of guests on board could not exceed 20, which was a ratio of crew to guest.

When I asked Captain Doug what his niche was, to me a rhetorical question, his response was not what I expected. He said that in all the years he has been taking guests out on reef tours, only a few have ever taken photos of the large tour boats cruising by, while his vessel — the only fully-functional operating former pearl farming boat — was a photo fan favorite. At well over 100 years old, being the only one of its kind offering Great Barrier Reef tours defines his niche and gives his company a competitive advantage over the larger tours.

Everyone and every company has a niche. Some are more obvious than others. If you have not yet defined yours, start by taking these three steps:

1. Make a list of things that make you or your company unique, then narrow this list down to two or three bullet points.

2. Ask other people to describe what makes you or your business different. Extract the aspects most listed by others.

3. Make a list of how your abilities are different from those of your colleagues, and why someone might choose you rather than another for assistance.

Describing your niche does not have to be paragraphs long, but it should allow you to be in a defensible position so that others cannot readily claim your niche as theirs. There may be subtle differences, but one or two words can make a tremendous difference in helping you to define, embrace, and optimize your personal or your company niche.

*This story is dedicated to Captain Dan and the crew of the Falla in Cairns, Australia.*

## Three Tips on Not Caring About What Others Think of You

*Why do you worry about what others think about you? Most likely they aren't, but if they were, what do you think they are really saying and why should it matter in the first place?*

I learned a long time ago, that it really doesn't matter what other people think about me, as long as I am confident and comfortable with the choices I make. Unfortunately, I don't think this attitude is very common. I also regularly speak with people about why they worry about others' opinions. This seems like an exhausting way to go through life, and it certainly is not productive. So why do so many people care about what others think of them?

Perhaps it's because they lack the confidence they should have to rise above and not concern themselves with others' perceptions. In fact, what other people think of you is really none of your business. What's more, it's likely not accurate, anyway. Most people are generally not good at being self-aware, let alone masters of the art of understanding why other people act the way they do.

Consider the last time you had some type of evaluation either by your boss, or informally by your family or significant other. Was their opinion and recent commentary about you completely accurate? I doubt it, and yet did you push back and ask them why they perceived you the way they did? In general, this would be considered aggressive behavior. Although there are exceptions, most people do not like confrontation.

If it is constructive information being shared in an appropriate manner, then it is acceptable behavior; however, if it is not, and is harmful and perhaps even destructive, it's best to step away.

If you are the type of person who is perpetually worried about what others think of you, then ask yourself these three questions:

1. Why am I so concerned with what other people think about me?
2. Why does it matter, and will it change anything?
3. Is being concerned about what others think of me a good use of my time and energy?

This last question is rhetorical, of course, and the answer is always *no*, so apply your time and energy towards someone or something more constructive.

Jot down five reasons you are awesome and read them aloud. If you can't think of five, ask a friend for help. I am amazed what I learn by doing this. Turns out I'm thoughtful, clever, loyal, genuine, and honest. This exercise will help divert you from negative thinking, and refocus you on why it does not matter what others are thinking about you.

Simply because you are convinced that others are thinking of you does not mean they are. Have you ever considered the fact that others, if they were thinking about you, might actually be thinking something positive? Why do we seem to have more of a tendency to assume others are only thinking negatively about us?

It is more important for you to spend your time and attention not caring what others are thinking, unless, of course, it is constructive feedback for which they've asked, or a compliment you wish to pay them.

I noticed a woman at my gym who was clearly trying to get in better shape and health. I had seen her there on a regular basis for about six months. During this time, she had probably lost well over 50 pounds. I was thinking how inspirational she has been to me on those days I did not want to work out, so I walked up to her and told her so. I complimented her on how fabulous she looked and told her to keep up the great work. She thanked me for telling her this, flashed a million-dollar smile, and said I made her day.

Can you stop caring about what others are thinking about you? Perhaps help someone else to do so, too? Think of how much better you and they will feel when you each focus your energy and thoughts on something worthy of your time and attention. Seriously, now go put this into practice.

# Five Tips on Electronic Etiquette

*It seems as if most people simply cannot live without their phones. Many appear to be addicted to communication devices. Here are my top five Smartphone etiquette guidelines.*

What is the one electronic gadget you always have on or near you? Most people will admit it's a phone, or some version of an device used to keep in touch with the rest of the world.

Thanks to technology, we are able to keep in touch 24/7 with virtually anyone else who is connected to a mobile communication device. There are clear advantages to this, but there is also a downside to always being available. It's easy to lose sight of the unwritten rules of electronic etiquette. Do you know what they are, or have you considered whether you might be breaking them?

I was surprised to find that *Forbes Magazine* last published an article in 2010 called *Top 10 Electronic Etiquette Faux Pas.* It covered a variety of electronic gadgets. The social blunders noted were reasonable and solutions exercised common sense. Focusing on our Smartphones, let's review five tips on how not to offend others. It's a safe bet that many of us have committed at least one offense in the last day or two! If applied, these guidelines could up the ante on our professional behavior to a whole new level of being polite as well as more aware and respectful of others.

1. No phones in the bathroom! Talking on the toilet or anywhere inside a public or private bathroom is a major faux pas. It is offensive on so many levels — hygiene being just one of them. I can't tell you how many toilets I have also heard flushing during conference call meetings. Just ... *no.*

2. Don't bring your phone to an interview, whether you are the interviewer or interviewee. It seems like common sense for the candidate to leave the phone behind and give 100 percent of his or her attention to the interviewer! I have also witnessed and been thoroughly disappointed by countless interviewers who have brought their phone to the interview, taken a call or two, and responded to

incoming texts while they were interviewing me or a candidate. Not only is this incredibly rude, it is disrespectful. Think twice about working for someone, or a company, who does not follow this rule.

3. Don't take calls or text when you are dining with others. Give the others at the table your their full attention. Take full advantage of this face-to-face interaction. If you are on your phone you are signaling to the rest of the guests that they are not as important as the attention you are giving to your Smartphone. Is this really the message you want to convey?

4. Your phone is not going to make you stronger when you talk on it at the gym. I am a big fan of listening to music or perhaps responding to texts or emails while on the treadmill, but it definitely is not a place I want to be hearing other people talking. Think about this the next time you queue up a phone conversation at the gym. Perhaps you didn't notice others glaring at you?

5. Don't bring your phone to meetings. The expectation is that you are there to be present and to contribute your full attention during the course of the discussion. When you are constantly checking your phone for incoming emails or responding to alerts, you are indicating that the people you are meeting with are not as important as your phone. You are also not able to devote your attention to what is being discussed, as you are distracted. Is this the message you intend to send?

There are numerous other rules that relate to using Smartphone in places or situations they should not, but these five should give you a great start to upping your phone etiquette. How many other examples of poor Smartphone etiquette can you add to the list?

## Know Your Audience — 11 Tips for Success

*Identifying your target audience and how to communicate with them seems like an obvious concept. But knowing and understanding your audience and which methods to use for optimum communications is where it gets complex.*

Ask yourself, "Do I know to whom am I speaking? What do they already know about my subject? What new information can I impart? What makes them tick?" The concept of knowing your audience may seem basic, but it is anything but simple. That's why when you present to an audience without planning, your communication may go in a different direction than intended.

Sales people tend to be the best at knowing and reading their audience, as they have a great deal of practice. As most of us are not in sales, or may not have as many opportunities to present to others, how do we become better at communicating to our audience? Here are 11 tips to better reading your audience and having your message successfully understood.

1. Don't make assumptions about how the audience will react. Remember the old, but wise, adage that defines the word *assume* as "not making an *ass* out of *you* and *me*."

2. If you do not know the people you will be addressing, simply ask their preferred methods of interacting. You may not be able to satisfy everyone, but you will have a better chance if you ask this question.

3. If you will be using visuals, make sure they don't break any best practice rules. Keep the number of words to an absolute minimum, and don't use graphics that are not coordinated with the message. After you have created the presentation, step away for a few minutes or overnight. Next time you view them, you will clearly see if they pass the "Keep It Simple" rule.

4. Actively invite the audience to hear what you have to say. Think back to grade school and how the teachers would always start with getting everyone's attention before they spoke. Ring a bell, if it's a light-hearted presentation. That will really set the tone, no pun intended.

5. Keep an eye on body language. If you speak too long, or do not allow interaction with you, you will likely lose rapt attention. If you see this happening, ask the audience if anyone has a question. If no one responds, pose a question someone should be asking.

6. When presenting to executives, be succinct. Tell them your "ask" up front, or announce the ideal outcome. When possible, keep your presentation to no more than 15 minutes. If you can't impart what you have to share in this period of time, chances are your message will not be impactful and provide the results you desire.

7. One-to-one conversations with people you know well may seem like the easiest audience, but again, the time, place, content, and your enthusiasm for your message can all play a role in a positive outcome.

8. Before you begin speaking, make sure you are in the right frame of mind. Think of yourself as if you were on stage. Would you start speaking in a monotone voice, with poor posture, eyes staring down, and with a lack energy? Of course not! Pretend you are an actor, if you have to. Before you know it, soon you'll come across enthusiastic about your topic. Attitudes are contagious – are yours worth catching?

9. When presenting to a live audience, make sure you are positioned so all can see and hear clearly. Ideally, if you are presenting visuals, stand at the front of the room. Many people make the mistake of sitting and miss the opportunity to command full attention.

10. If you do not know your audience well, do some basic research. If it's a single person, check them out on LinkedIn, read their bios on their company website, or Google and see what you find. If possible, ask others that know them well to provide you with the inside scoop on how they prefer to receive information.

11. Bonus tip! After the meeting, send a "thanks for attending" note and a summary of the information presented. Keep it short, and leverage this communication to convey your key points. Now that you have some tips on how to know your audience, go out and start putting them into action.

## Five Tips on Improving Communication

*How well you have honed your communication skills will ultimately determine the direction in which your career is headed and the professional level you reach. Being aware of the communication faux pas you may be making is crucial to business success. The good news is that you can always work on enhancing your skills that put your career on a new path forward.*

Almost daily people ask me for advice on how to improve upon their communication skills, the communications between them and another colleague, or the skill set of a team they work with or manage. Since there are varying degrees of how well people communicate interpersonally, or with multiple types of personalities, there is typically a range of how well information is being interpreted and whether messages are being clearly conveyed, or not. For some people, the ability to communicate effectively is a natural talent, but for most, it is a skill that needs continuous work to obtain a basic to intermediate level of proficiency.

It is obvious when you come across someone who has mastered the art of communicating well. You can appreciate how smoothly they are able to transfer information. Conversely, we have all experienced having to interact with others who lack basic communciation skills.

So, what can you do if you are challenged, or when you must deal with people who are not at your same level? Here are some tips you can consider putting into practice.

- Five Ws and an H: Ask the person to cover what in journalism school is referred to as the "Five Ws and an H" — Who, What, When, Where, Why and How. Typically, when one of these elements is left out, it leaves room for misinterpretation and elongates the process of getting the message across.

- Time Line: Whether you are interacting with one person or a large group, it is important to make sure everyone is aware of whether the topic has a time line for follow up. Not all do, but when it does and this is not articulated, communications break down.

- Methods of Communicating: Simply because you like to talk, does not mean everyone does. Some people prefer to communicate in writing, or in a combination of face-to-face, phone, and correspondence. It's simple! Just ask and agree on the person or groups' preferred method(s) of communication.

- Formal vs. Informal: Depending on with whom you are communicating, the topic, how well you know the person, or a myriad of other factors will contribute to whether it is more effective to use a formal or informal style. It is best to lean towards the formal at first. As the conversations continue, notice during the course of conversations whether the recipient modifies the style to the less formal and then follow suit.

- Don't Make Assumptions: If you are not clear about an aspect of the communication, ask for clarification. You can do this with either the entire group, or with one to two people involved in the discussion. You can ask them privately to see if they interpreted the information the same way you did. If everyone is confused, it may be time to stop and refocus on either the time line, or the Five Ws and an H.

Practicing your communication skills may not be your idea of fun, but the stronger you become at communicating and modeling communication skills in meetings, the easier it will be for you to interact with your boss, colleagues and everyone else you meet.

Not sure where you stand on the communication scale? Ask two or three people you know well, respect, and from whom you would be comfortable receiving constructive feedback. It is important to ask them to only give constructive feedback on areas for improvement, and to also share with you aspects of how you communicate well.

If you work on the feedback, ask if they would be willing to re-evaluate your progress in another month. This will give you plenty of time to practice and hone the skills you desire, and focus on the opportunities you will have when you are at a higher level of being able to converse effectively with others.

## Six Tips for Making the Most of Lunch and Learns

*Lunch and Learns offer a casual atmosphere for learning. But they're also critical to future professional opportunities. Learn how to make the most of this educational format.*

When I first heard the phrase "lunch and learn" I thought, "Great: Less time to eat and digest my food; more time listening to someone drone on about a topic I likely can't relate to, or have little to zero interest in hearing about."

I know this sounds like a terrible attitude; it was. What I soon realized, though, was how important these sessions are from both a learning and performance perspective. I soon learned that the concept is a great way to learn about something I likely might not readily learn about on my own. But I also discovered wide variations in how well or poorly these sessions were presented. When they were done well, I walked away feeling refreshed, having been graced with new knowledge. Conversely, when the topic was presented poorly, or did not take into consideration who was in the audience, the experience felt painful and pointless.

Not all companies take advantage of these informal learning sessions, but the ones that do, and do them well, provide both the audience and presenter with an amazing opportunity for career development. The presenter can polish his or her presentation skills, while the audience is introduced to a topic they may not otherwise have the opportunity to learn about.

The most effective sessions limit the presentation time to 30 minutes, including Q&A. Providing the audience with an opportunity to interact significantly enhances the session, and makes it easier for the attendees to consume the information.

Volunteering to present a Lunch and Learn might seem reserved for those at the senior level, but this is not true. Having a mixture of staff with different career experience makes these sessions more appealing, and also serves as a way of having more employees at different levels actively engaged in the company. Providing an opportunity for less-seasoned employees to present to those with more career years under their belts is also a fantastic way for veterans to feel comfortable learning from their peers or subordinates. For more senior employees, Lunch and Learns offer an opportunity to share knowledge with others and appear more approachable down the line, as the audience will feel like they know the person slightly better from the experience.

For those afraid of speaking in public, Lunch and Learns are a great way to make public speaking something you can look forward to instead of dreading. Since the format is fairly casual, and the majority of companies do not put many restrictions around what or how to present the material, everyone should accept the challenge of presenting at a Lunch and Learn.

If your company does not offer them, talk to someone in human resources or on your marketing team about helping you to organize the first one. If your firm is small and you do not have someone in either of these roles, take it upon yourself to approach company leadership with the idea.

Here's what you can tell them about the value of these sessions:

1. Lunch and Learns provide a relaxed learning opportunity for all employees, and if the boss treats for lunch, it provides good karma points for the management team.

2. Everyone has an opportunity to learn from a colleague versus having someone from the outside having to come in to teach.

3. Giving employees a platform to practice speaking and presentation skills is something almost every company should do, but usually, finding the opportunity is a challenge.

4. Sessions can serve as a way to have employees from different departments bond through a common interest in the topic being presented.

5. Supporting Lunch and Learns shows that a company is interested in the development of its employees. It is not only effective, it's cost-effective, too.

6. Don't be just a "seat warmer;" take advantage of being a speaker, too. Doing so could provide you with more exposure to others in the company who may be one of your future bosses.

# 10 Ways to Determine If You're a Secret Entrepreneur

*Since I come from a long line of inventors and entrepreneurs, I assume that being an entrepreneur is in my DNA. But everyone has the ability to be one, if they are so inclined. Do you have what it takes to work for yourself?*

My grandfather worked with Dr. Edwin H. Land, the inventor of the Polaroid Land camera and film, and my uncle was the first architect to design and build a million-dollar home in Massachusetts. My brother runs his own company. Even though I'd worked for a number of companies over the years, I always felt compelled to work for myself. Sound familiar? Perhaps you have considered this on an especially frustrating day at work, or when you feel as if you are a proverbial cog-in-a-wheel, or a hamster spinning 'round and 'round and getting nowhere, fast.

If you find yourself dreading Mondays then maybe it's time to start thinking about whether being self-employed might be an option. Of course, the security of having health insurance is one of the main reasons most people don't consider leaving the Mother Ship. Benefits such as a steady salary, a 401K plan, paid vacation, life insurance, and other perks are certainly hard to walk away from.

But there are perks that come with working for yourself, too: You are the boss and get to decide how to grow your company. And you will know that you can support yourself financially and be independent, or are making a difference with the service or product you provide.

Careful planning and research into whether the idea of being an entrepreneur makes economic sense could be the catalyst you need to consider this employment route. So consider these 10 steps before you begin drafting that resignation letter.

1. Create a timeline to embark upon your entrepreneurial journey.

2. Is your service, product, or concept unique, or something offered by others? If it is similar to other companies, what will make you stand out from the competition and be economically viable?

3. Put together a budget to see how much savings you will need to begin striking out on your own.

4. Develop a business plan that outlines what you will be doing, your go-to-market-plan, how you will make money, and in what time frame, as well as your actual and projected expenses.

5. To determine whether your value proposition is battle ready to merit investment from a venture capitalist, pretend you are going to pitch your company on Shark Tank. Deliver your pitch to a mirror until it feels comfortable and real.

6. Develop a fallback plan. Build an out clause into your business plan in the event you get to the point it makes more sense to hit the eject button before you are in an unrecoverable position.

7. Create and nurture a business and personal network for support and advice on how to handle situations with which you are not experienced.

8. Join networking groups or Chambers of Commerce. Many are willing to give complimentary advice, or even barter for your product or services. Some of these connections may become members of your Board of Advisors.

9. Choose people in your network for advice essential to running the business. Consider which skills you will need to grow your business. One of the key elements entrepreneurs need is a strong sense of how to market and sell their company. If these are not talents you possess, either start learning, or ask others for help.

10. Research how other entrepreneurs have made mistakes. Ask them to share how to avoid the early and elementary mistakes they made. You do not have to re-create the wheel when it comes to being an entrepreneur, so be open to taking advice from those who have had success.

Does the appeal of being an entrepreneur seem better on paper as a concept, or do you feel, as I did, compelled to try this employment route? If you can't stop thinking about being an entrepreneur, then maybe it's time for you to start making plans! Harness and then leverage the energy and enthusiasm you have, and go for it.

## Six Tips on How to Unplug and Recharge Yourself

*Allocating down time is critical to both productivity, and more importantly, your well-being. Too many people get caught in the trap of not taking time to recharge. Some employees are afraid to take time off, concerned that they will either miss out on big news, or be penalized. This type of thinking is both paralyzing and short-sighted. Learn how to step off the merry-go-round and start gaining the benefits associated with unplugging.*

Humans need to take breaks. Studies show that after recharging, we all perform far better and are more creative and productive. It never ceases to amaze me when people boast that they never take breaks or vacations and work all the time. What further astounds me is that they think that is a badge of honor. They are actually fooling themselves into thinking they are always highly productive. It is impossible to be at peak performance all of the time, especially when you do not take any breaks.

The U.S. has earned a reputation for living to work versus other countries who embrace the concept of working to live. Granted, there are factors that make it more challenging to adopt the "working to live" frame of mind, but we can still increase the quality of our lives by taking more breaks, whether they are mental, physical, or both.

People in other countries have figured out the balance and learned to infuse down time into their schedules. Why do so many Americans pride themselves by acting like robots and not taking the down time they need or have earned? One challenge in the U.S. is employees typically have only a few weeks of vacation time each year, three if they are lucky, and four if they are even more fortunate. Studies show that even when people have earned or accumulated that much vacation time, most of them either do not use it, or are concerned about actually taking a break. This is a shame, as both physical health and mental wellbeing are compromised.

So, how do we learn to embrace down time? Below are a few suggestions on how to feel more comfortable taking time off, or working some down time into each and every day.

1. Every few hours, get up and walk around. Yes, literally walk around your office, or go outside to get some fresh air. Changing your environment even for a short period of time can help you to recharge, particularly when the sun is out and you get to experience it in person and not by viewing it from the inside out.

2. Take a coffee or lunch break. At first, you might be tempted to incorporate some of your work into this time, but slowly ease yourself out of doing this habit (or practice).

3. If you are near a retail store, take a trip simply to look around and take a visual vacation from what you are thinking about or looking at most of the day. You'll be pleasantly surprised how refreshed you'll feel when you get back to the task at hand.

4. Plan a vacation or staycation. Having something to look forward to is a great way to be more inspired about your work. After you take the actual break, you will feel like a new person again. Sometimes just three days of either doing something other than work, or fully relaxing can put you in a much better frame of mind. Be amazed at the increased productivity when you return, refreshed and raring to go again.

5. Consider picking up a new hobby or an interest potentially using your down time to volunteer your time and skills. Participating in a fun activity and helping others offer tremendous benefits in helping your mind and body to refuel.

6. Learning how to meditate is also something you can do both at work and at home. Many highly successful business people have turned to meditation to recalibrate, enhance overall well-being, and become more productive. Meditate for as little as five minutes and feel the positive results. Everyone has at least five minutes per day to spare, so give this a try. In fact, schedule it right into your calendar.

Everyone has a choice of how to use their time. It is a matter of making time to recharge a priority. You are worth it.

## 10 Ways to Boost Your Powers of Observation

*It never ceases to amaze me how many people are unaware of their surroundings. How can they not pay attention to what is going on at work, on the highway, or even at home? Learn how you can turn the power of observation into positive opportunities.*

Have you ever had a day when you feel as if you cannot focus or pay attention? You are not alone. More and more people have claimed they have Attention Deficit Disorder — which they might, but I suspect they are instead overstimulated (or overwhelmed) by their environment.

Noticing everything that surrounds you seems like an obvious survival technique. Since we have become more reliant on electronic gadgets and gizmos, however, many people have seemed to have lost their observational skills. Indeed, being aware of your surroundings should be second nature. But if you feel unsure whether you have mastered this skill or not, becoming more observant will serve you well in many situations. Below are five questions to assess whether you are an observant person, or have a long way to go.

- Do people routinely ask if you are paying attention, or listening?
- Do colleagues seldom ask for your opinion on work matters?
- Do you find yourself sometimes unaware of what is going on around you?
- Are you surprised more often than not by the opinions of others?
- Do you get caught off-guard by questions asked by others, when they expect you to know the answers?

If you can relate to any of the points above, tap into my 10 techniques to help you become more observant. People will perceive you differently and in a more positive manner.

1. Pay attention to how people react to your conversations. If they are not asking questions and fully engaging with you, this could be because they do not think you are paying full attention to them.

2. Are you talking about yourself too much and not asking the people

around you questions about themselves? People who are less observant tend not to ask others many questions.

3. Do other people only have brief conversations with you? If the majority of your chats are short, this could signal that others assume you are insincere or not engaged enough with the interaction to warrant going beyond a quick, casual conversation.

4. Always ask the people with whom you meet how they are doing. Pay attention to their words and their body language. Make sure your responses are sincere.

5. When you are communicating with others in an open area, make sure your voice is at an appropriate level, and not distracting to others. Some people are completely unaware of their voice level being too loud. This is not only inconsiderate, but others will perceive you as being unaware of your surroundings.

6. Might your interactions appear to be confrontational? This could be because you are not observing whether it is an ideal time to interact. For example, it is late Friday afternoon and you are talking to a someone about something that could or should have been handled earlier in the week.

7. Are your time management skills in question? Have you noticed that you are not on pace with your co-workers?

8. Ask a few people you trust for feedback on how they would rate your observational skills. On a scale of one to five, with five being highly observational, if you score a three or less, see the next question.

9. If you are not perceived as being observational, ask the people who rated you for some reasons. What did they observe?

10. Ask those who rated your skills for suggestions on how you could be better at observing your surroundings, and then put them into practice. A few weeks later, ask these same people if they would change your rating.

Becoming more observant will serve you well. It's easy and rewarding to become aware of your surroundings — it just takes practice!

# | Bibliography |

Buzan, Tony and Buzan, Barry. *The Mind Map Book: How to Use Radiant Thinking to Maximize Your Brain's Untapped Potential.* New York: Plume, 1996.

D, Peter. Life of Privilege Explained in a $100 Race. Published on YouTube, October 14, 2017. Retrieved from https://www.youtube.com/watch?v=4K5fbQ1-zps

Ferrazzi, Keith. *Never Eat Alone: And Other Secrets to Success, One Relationship at a Time.* New York: Crown Business, 2005.

Fox, Justin. "Instinct Can Beat Analytical Thinking." *Harvard Business Review.* June 20, 2014. Retrieved from https://hbr.org/2014/06/instinct-can-beat-analytical-thinking

Gelb, Michael J. *Lessons From The Art Of Juggling: How to Achieve Your Full Potential in Business, Learning, and Life.* New York: Three Rivers Press, 1994.

Kahneman, Daniel. *Thinking, Fast and Slow.* New York: Farrar, Straus and Giroux, 2011.

Loesser, Frank. "I Believe in You." *How to Succeed in Business Without Really Trying.* October 14, 1961: 46th Street Theatre, New York, NY

Macabasco, Lou. "6 Effective Ways to Become Persistent." LifeHack.org. Retrieved from https://www.lifehack.org/articles/productivity/6-effective-ways-to-become-persistent.html

Monte, Maureen Electa. *Destination Unstoppable.* Michigan: Maureen Monte Consulting, LLC, 2016.

Oracles, The. "11 Genius Tips to Be More Decisive." *Success Magazine.* January 31, 2017. Retrieved from https://www.success.com/article/11-genius-tips-to-be-more-decisive

Pasek, Ben; Paul, Justin; and Levenson, Steven; directed by Michael Greif. "Dear Evan Hansen." New York: Grand Central Publishing, 2017.

Peale, Dr. Norman Vincent. *The Power of Positive Thinking.* Arkansas: Fireside Books, 2007. (First Published 1952)

Rath, Tom. *Strengths Finder 2.0.* Washington, DC: Gallup Press, 2007.

Tolle, Eckhart. *The Power of Now: A Guide to Spiritual Enlightenment.* Novato (CA): New World Library, 2004.

Winters, Elizabeth Anne. "Top 10 Electronic Etiquette Faux Pas." *Forbes Magazine.* November 11, 2010. Retrieved from https://www.forbes.com/2010/11/11/technology-electronic-etiquette-forbes-woman-leadership-social-media.html#35e6b6a0e9ad